REGIMENTAL NICKNAMES AND TRADITIONS OF THE BRITISH ARMY
BY
Anonymous

REGIMENTAL NICKNAMES AND TRADITIONS OF THE BRITISH ARMY

Published by Wallachia Publishers

New York City, NY

First published 1916

Copyright © Wallachia Publishers, 2015

All rights reserved

Except in the United States of America, this book is sold subject to the condition that it shall not, by way of trade or otherwise, be lent, re-sold, hired out, or otherwise circulated without the publisher's prior consent in any form of binding or cover other than that in which it is published and without a similar condition including this condition being imposed on the subsequent purchaser.

ABOUT WALLACHIA PUBLISHERS

Wallachia Publishers mission is to publish the world's finest European history texts. More information on our recent publications and catalog can be found on our website.

Preface to 1st Edition

When the Territorial System was adopted in 1881, the old titles borne by our regiments were, in many cases, changed, and in other instances entirely lost. When the old titles changed, the Nicknames, by which nearly every corps was known, disappeared. These Nicknames often brought to mind some amusing event or memorable incident in the regiment's career, and in many cases originated from some peculiarity in the uniform, or, in the case of a cavalry regiment, the colour of the horses. There is no official record kept of these Nicknames, as they were wholly unrecognised by the "Army List"; it is, therefore, hoped that the record of the old names and titles as shown in this work will be appreciated.

FORMER TITLES OF THE BATTALIONS OF INFANTRY

Late Regiment	Present Title Abbreviated
1st Foot	R. Scots
2nd "	R. W. Surrey R.
3rd "	E. Kent R.
4th "	R. Lanc. R.
5th "	Northd. Fus.
6th "	R. War. R.
7th "	R. Fus.
8th "	L'pool R.
9th "	Norf. R.
10th "	Linc. R.
11th "	Devon R.
12th "	Suff. R.
13th "	Som. L. I.
14th "	W. York R.
15th "	E. York R.
16th "	Bedf. Reg.
17th "	Leic. R.
18th "	R. Ir. Regt.
19th "	York R.
20th "	Lanc. Fus.
21st "	R. Sc. Fus.
22nd "	Ches. R.
23rd "	R. W. Fus.

24th "	S. Wales Bord.
25th "	K. O. S. B.
26th "	1st Bn. Sco. Rif.
27th "	1st Bn. R. Innis. Fus.
28th "	1st Bn. Glouc. R.
29th "	1st Bn. Worc. R.
30th "	1st Bn. E. Lanc. R.
31st "	1st Bn. E. Surr. R.
32nd "	1st Bn. D. of Corn. L. I.
33rd "	1st Bn. W. Rid. R.
34th "	1st Bn. Bord. R.
35th "	1st Bn. R. Suss. R.
36th "	2nd Bn. Worc. R.
37th "	1st Bn. Hants. R.
38th "	1st Bn. S. Staff. R.
39th "	1st Bn. Dorset R.
40th "	1st Bn. S. Lan. R.
41st "	1st Bn. Welsh R.
42nd "	1st Bn. R. Highrs.
43rd "	1st Bn. Oxf. & Bucks L. I.
44th "	1st Bn. Essex R.
45th "	1st Bn. Notts. & Derby R.
46th "	2nd Bn. D. of Corn. L. I.
47th "	1st Bn. N. Lanc. R.
48th "	1st Bn. North'n R.
49th "	1st Bn. R. Berks R.
50th "	1st Bn. R. W. Kent R.
51st "	1st Bn. Yorks L. I.

52nd "	2nd Bn. Oxf. & Bucks L. I.
53rd "	1st Bn. Shrops. L. I.
54th "	2nd Bn. Dorset R.
55th "	2nd Bn. Bord. R.
56th "	2nd Bn. Essex R.
57th "	1st Bn. Midd'x R.
58th "	2nd Bn. North'n. R.
59th "	2nd Bn. E. Lanc. R.
60th "	K. R. R. C.
61st "	2nd Bn. Glouc. R.
62nd "	1st Bn. Wilts. R.
63rd "	1st Bn. Manch. R.
64th "	1st Bn. N. Staff. R.
65th "	1st Bn. Y. and L. R.
66th "	2nd Bn. R. Berks R.
67th "	2nd Bn. Hants R.
68th "	1st Bn. Durh. L. I.
69th "	2nd Bn. Welsh R.
70th "	2nd Bn. E. Surr. R.
71st "	1st Bn. High. L. I.
72nd "	1st Bn. Sea. Highrs.
73rd "	2nd Bn. R. Highrs.
74th "	2nd Bn. High. L. I.
75th "	1st Bn. Gord. Highrs.
76th "	2nd Bn. W. Rid. R.
77th "	2nd Bn. Midd'x R.
78th "	2nd Bn. Sea. Highrs.
79th "	1st Bn. Cam. Highrs.

80th "	2nd Bn. S. Staff. R.
81st "	2nd Bn. N. Lan. R.
82nd "	2nd Bn. S. Lan. R.
83rd "	1st Bn. R. Ir. Rif.
84th "	2nd Bn. Y. and L. R.
85th "	2nd Bn. Shrops. L. I.
86th "	2nd Bn. R. Ir. Rif.
87th "	1st Bn. R. Ir. Fus.
88th "	1st Bn. Conn. Rang.
89th "	2nd Bn. R. Ir. Fus.
90th "	2nd Bn. Sco. Rif.
91st "	1st Bn. A. and S. Highrs.
92nd "	2nd Bn. Gord. Highrs.
93rd "	2nd Bn. A. and S. Highrs.
94th "	2nd Bn. Conn. Rang.
95th "	2nd Bn. Notts. & Derby R.
96th "	2nd Bn. Manch. R.
97th "	2nd Bn. R. W. Kent R.
98th "	2nd Bn. N. Staff. R.
99th "	2nd Bn. Wilts. R.
100th "	1st Bn. Leins. R.
101st "	1st Bn. R. Muns. Fus.
102nd "	1st Bn. R. Dub. Fus.
103rd "	2nd Bn. R. Dub. Fus.
104th "	2nd Bn. R. Muns. Fus.
105th "	2nd Bn. Yorks L. I.
106th "	2nd Bn. Durh. L. I.
107th "	2nd Bn. R. Suss. R.

108th "	2nd Bn. R. Innis. Fus.
109th "	2nd Bn. Leins. R.
Rifle Brigade	Rif. Brig.

FOREWORD

The sudden expansion of the British Army to a strength undreamed of prior to August, 1914, brought in its train an ever-increasing desire on the part of the public for a better knowledge of the Army and of its glorious traditions, a subject that had previously attracted little or no attention outside military circles. Even among an average body of soldiers there is curiously enough a lack of knowledge of military history outside that closely associated with their own regiment. Yet the history of the British Army is unequalled by any other in the world for splendid achievement, while the regimental histories and traditions teem with instances of devotion to duty, gallantry in the face of overwhelming odds, and self-sacrifice of the most glorious nature. These traditions are highly treasured in the regiments, and their preservation has tended to build up and sustain in each unit that splendid *esprit de corps* which has animated all ranks, and made almost the impossible possible to our gallant soldiers in the presence of hardships and danger, and has led them to face death with a courage and heroism unsurpassed in the history of the world.

The traditions of the British Army stretch back over four centuries, during which it has been the acknowledged means of winning and building up the greatest Empire the world has ever known. The Army's deeds are a sealed book so far as the general public are concerned, for military matters except in times of actual war have never been a popular subject, the great heroes of the battlefield being far less known to the British public than popular performers on the football field or pampered professional boxers.

THE ROMANCE OF MILITARY HISTORY

The history of the British Army is full of romance and interest and many curious customs, incidents and observances are associated with most of the regiments. Each regiment has peculiarities of custom which it has made its own by long use, besides winning unofficial titles and nicknames commemorative of some deed of daring or peculiarity of dress or tradition. The following pages deal with these, and if in perusing them the reader is encouraged to learn more of the glorious history and traditions of the British Army, which he will do with increasing satisfaction and interest, the author will feel amply rewarded.

Although outwardly all regiments or battalions of one branch of the service are alike to the ordinary observer, there are, however, many little differences distinguishing them. These little differences are for the most part the sole remaining links with those gallant regiments of the past from which they have descended, and whose glorious achievements are a subject of great pride to all ranks. For instance, in the Royal Artillery there may be no difference to be detected between the various batteries or companies, yet each has traditions and subtle differences highly prized, as for instance the Chestnut Troop, the Rocket Troop, and the Battleaxe Company, all reminiscent of glorious incidents in their history.

CAVALRY DISTINCTIONS

The Household Cavalry are now the only British Cavalry still wearing the polished steel cuirass. Yet each of the regiments has little differences apparent only to the close observer. Thus, the 1st Life Guards wear a red cord as their shoulder belts and black sheep-skins on their saddles, the 2nd Life Guards wearing a blue cord and white sheep-skins. The seven regiments of Dragoon Guards differ somewhat from each other in point of uniform. They, with the Royal Engineers, are the only regiments in the army to wear velvet facings. Their helmets are of brass, the helmets of the Household Cavalry and Dragoons being of white metal. The three regiments of Dragoons are representative of England, Scotland and Ireland, being the 1st Royal Dragoons, Royal Scots Greys and Inniskilling Dragoons, the Greys being distinctive by reason of the colour of their horses and their bearskin head-dress.

Each of the twelve regiments of Hussars, introduced into the service in 1806 as Light Dragoons, has also certain distinctions of dress, as also have the six regiments of Lancers, the best known of which is perhaps the 17th Lancers on account of its grim crest, a skull with crossbones, which, with its motto "Or Glory" has led to its popular name of "The Death or Glory Boys." It is an interesting fact that the 17th Lancers in 1795 provided a detachment for service on H.M.S. "Hermione" as Marines, and were promptly nicknamed "The Horse Marines." Lancer regiments were introduced into the British Army in 1816.

Each regiment of Dragoon Guards carries a standard on ceremonial occasions, and Dragoon regiments carry a guidon (a swallow-tailed standard). Hussar and Lancer regiments do not carry standards, bearing their battle honours on their appointments.

PRIVILEGES OF THE FOOT GUARDS

The regiments of Foot Guards, known as the Brigade of Guards, have many privileges and duties reserved to them alone. They claim the privilege of guarding the Royal Palaces and form part of the Household Troops of the Sovereign. The First Company of the 1st Battalion Grenadier Guards is known as the King's Company and is comprised of picked men of particularly fine physique, none under 6 feet in height being admitted to it. This company has the right to carry on parade on state and ceremonial occasions a colour of crimson silk, the gift of the Sovereign, being the only company in the Army so privileged. The First Company of the Welsh Guards, formed in 1915, is known as The Prince of Wales's Company, and is also composed of picked men. The Scots Guards is the only regular Scottish regiment to have drum and fife bands. The Quartermasters of the Brigade of Guards wear cocked hats with plumes, the Grenadier and Scots Guards, white; the Coldstream Guards, red; and the Irish Guards, blue. The sergeant-majors of the Foot Guards wear an elaborate Royal Coat of Arms on their right sleeves above the elbow.

No chevrons or badges are worn by staff-sergeants of the Foot Guards in undress uniform.

The Royal or King's Colour in regiments of Foot Guards is of crimson silk, and bears the distinctions conferred by Royal authority. The regimental colour of Foot Guards is the Union Jack, and battle honours are borne on both colours. The King's Colour of the Infantry of the Line is the Union Jack, with the regimental badge superimposed, but the regimental colour is distinctive in each regiment and the battle honours are borne on these alone.

PIPERS' PECULIARITIES

Regarding pipers it is a curious fact that the Regulations provide for an issue of fifes to Scottish regiments but not bagpipes, which have to be provided regimentally, although with the exception of the Scots Guards, the fifes are never drawn from stores. In the Royal Scots, Royal Scots Fusiliers, King's Own Scottish Borderers and Scottish Rifles, pipers are officially borne on the strength, but no clothing allowed for them, which has to be provided regimentally. The sergeant-pipers of the Scots Guards alone wear a crown and silver chevrons on their doublet sleeves, all other sergeant-pipers wearing gold chevrons without a crown.

There are many interesting peculiarities connected with uniforms or accoutrements. The Kilmarnock bonnets worn by the Royal Scots and King's Own Scottish Borderers, which were designed and issued for wear after the South African War, are quite distinctive, as also are the chacos of the Scottish Rifles and Highland Light Infantry, the former having a plume in front and the latter a ball. The Queen's Royal West Surrey Regiment is the only regiment in the Army wearing a sacred emblem as a badge, while the Buffs (East Kent Regiment) claim to have a far more ancient lineage than any other English regiment.

ANIMAL BADGES

The King's Own Royal Lancaster Regiment wears the Lion of England for a badge, and it is interesting to note that many other regiments go to the animal kingdom for their crests, the Royal Warwickshire Regiment wearing an antelope as a badge; the King's Liverpool Regiment, West Yorkshire Regiment and Royal West Kent Regiment, a horse; the Buffs, the Scottish Rifles, Royal Berkshire Regiment, North Staffordshire Regiment and York and Lancaster Regiment, a dragon; the Gordon Highlanders, Royal Munster Fusiliers, Royal Dublin Fusiliers, Leicestershire Regiment and Hampshire Regiment, a tiger; the West Riding Regiment, Connaught Rangers, Seaforth Highlanders, and the Highland Light Infantry, an elephant; the Royal Irish Fusiliers, an eagle; the Argyll and Sutherland Highlanders, a cat; and the Bedfordshire Regiment, a stag.

QUICK STEPPING INFANTRY

The Light Infantry regiments wear a bugle or French horn as part of their badge, and together with Rifle regiments march with a much quicker step than do other infantry regiments. The regulation pace is 120 to the minute, but Rifle and Light Infantry regiments step much quicker, 140 to 160, except when marching with other troops, then their pace is that laid down for the army generally. They have bugle bands instead of drum and fife bands.

The Northumberland Fusiliers are the only regiment to celebrate St. George's Day, and are looked upon as the representative English infantry regiment in the British Army and their crest of St. George and the Dragon is unique.

All Fusilier regiments wear sealskin fusilier caps with distinctive plumes, and a grenade as a badge. The Royal Fusiliers is best known as the City of London Regiment, and has some peculiar privileges in consequence, one of these being the right to march through the City of London with fixed bayonets, colours flying, and drums beating, without first obtaining the permission of the Lord Mayor and Aldermen. This privilege is shared by the Buffs, the Grenadier Guards and Royal Marines only.

The Norfolk Regiment has a curious crest, being the figure of Britannia as it used to appear on the copper coinage, and is the only regiment not having a Royal title, of which His Majesty is Colonel-in-Chief. The Lincolnshire Regiment was for some years after being raised the only British regiment of infantry to wear blue coats.

THE MINDEN REGIMENTS

The Suffolk Regiment was one of the six regiments of British infantry that performed the remarkable feat of charging and utterly destroying a column of French cavalry, superior in numbers to themselves. This was at Minden, the other five regiments being the Lancashire Fusiliers, Royal Welsh Fusiliers, King's Own Scottish Borderers, Hampshire Regiment and the Yorkshire Light Infantry. The regiments passed to the battlefield through gardens of roses in full bloom, and the soldiers picked the blossoms and fixed them in their hats, and in commemoration of their victory they enjoy the right of wearing roses in their head-dress on the anniversary of the battle.

The Prince Albert's Somerset Light Infantry has two peculiar distinctions, one being that it is the only regiment without a Royal title to wear blue for its facings, and the other being that the sergeants enjoy the right of wearing their sashes over the left shoulder the same as the officers, in commemoration of their devoted gallantry at the battle of Culloden, when the casualties among the officers were so numerous that the sergeants were left in command.

The Cheshire Regiment also enjoys a peculiar privilege, that of wearing oak leaves in its head-dress and as a wreath on its colour staves on all Royal ceremonial parades, in commemoration of its rally round its Sovereign who took shelter at a critical moment beneath an oak tree during the battle of Dettingen.

WELSH TRADITIONS

Among the peculiarities of the Royal Welsh Fusiliers is that of wearing a bunch of black ribbons fastened to the back of the collar. This is a survival of the patch of black leather which in former days was worn by all soldiers on the back to prevent the grease from the powdered pigtails from soiling the tunics. The regiment also enjoys the privilege, common to all Welsh regiments, of being led on parade by a goat, these animals being generally gifts from the Sovereign.

The South Wales Borderers have a highly-prized distinction, that of bearing a silver wreath of immortelles fastened to their King's colour, in commemoration of the devoted bravery of the regiment in the Zulu War.

All the Welsh regiments carry on their colours, or as badges, the device of the Plume of the Prince of Wales, the Rising Sun, and the Red Dragon of Cadwaladr.

The Royal Inniskilling Fusiliers were for many years the only regiment in the British Army using the old Irish war pipes, but now other Irish regiments have adopted the custom and possess full pipe bands. The Irish war pipe has but two drones, as distinctive from the Scottish bagpipes which have three.

THE GLORY OF THE GLOUCESTERS AND WORCESTERS

The Gloucestershire Regiment has a unique distinction, that of wearing a miniature replica of its badge at the back of its head-dress, bestowed for its gallantry at the battle of Alexandria, when being suddenly attacked front and rear simultaneously, the rear ranks of the regiment turned about and beat the enemy off.

The Worcestershire Regiment has as its motto the word "Firm," bestowed for steadiness in the face of the foe, and naturally highly prized.

The Duke of Wellington's West Riding Regiment enjoys two peculiar distinctions, the first that of being the only regiment in the British Army bearing the name of anyone except a Royal personage as part of its title, and also of being the only regiment to wear scarlet facings to its red tunics.

THE BORDERS' UNIQUE HONOUR

The Border Regiment alone among the regiments of the Army bears the battle honour of "Arroyo dos Molinos," although a number of regiments took part in that great battle.

The Welsh Regiment, like the Welsh Guards, has a motto in the Welsh language. The former served with distinction as marines on board the fleet under Lord Nelson.

The Black Watch wears a red hackle or feather in its bonnets, a distinction won on the battlefield, and its pipers are the only ones in the army wearing feather bonnets instead of glengarry caps.

THE GREENJACKETS

The King's Royal Rifle Corps and the Rifle Brigade are known as the Greenjackets, from the colour of their full dress uniform, and like all Rifle regiments wear fur busbies. They do not carry colours, their battle honours being emblazoned on their appointments. They do not carry their rifles at the slope but at the trail. There are two other Rifle regiments in the British Army, these being the Scottish Rifles (The Cameronians) and the Royal Irish Rifles.

THE ELEPHANT COLOURS.

The Highland Light Infantry and Seaforth Highlanders enjoy the privilege of carrying a third colour on parade, this having been presented to them to commemorate their bravery at the battle of Assaye, and being emblazoned with an elephant is known as the Assaye or Elephant Colour. The Seaforth is the only regiment to have a Gaelic motto.

The Queen's Own Cameron Highlanders have a larger proportion of Gaelic-speaking soldiers in their ranks than any other, most of them hailing from the most northern part of the Highlands.

BATTLE HONOURS.

Before the great war on the Continent the King's Royal Rifle Corps were credited with the highest number of battle honours, viz., 40, the Gloucester Regiment being second with 34, then in order the Rifle Brigade 33, Highland Light Infantry 32, Black Watch and Gordon Highlanders 31 each, Royal Welsh Fusiliers, Royal Scots, South Staffordshire Regiment and South Lancashire Regiment 29 each, Oxfordshire and Buckinghamshire Light Infantry 27, Sherwood Foresters, Seaforth Highlanders, Royal Munster Fusiliers, Northamptonshire Regiment and Royal Dublin Fusiliers 25 each, and The Buffs, East Surrey Regiment and Grenadier Guards 24 each. The 16th Lancers have the highest number of honours amongst the Cavalry regiments, viz., 18, the 9th Lancers having 16, and the 14th Hussars 15.

Many other matters of interest attaching to each regiment will be found in the following pages.

Royal Escort of Life Guards at St. James's Palace.
Types of Royal Flying Corps Aeroplanes and Anti-Aircraft Gun

(*Record Office*, Aldershot)
Uniform, Blue.
Facings, Scarlet.
Service Uniform, Khaki fold-over jacket, breeches, and putties, with turndown cap.
Motto: *Per Ardua ad Astra* (Through difficulties to the Stars).

Qualified Pilot's Badge worn on left breast

ROYAL FLYING CORPS

The great European war brought out in startling fashion the remarkable efficiency of the military aerial service, which is embodied in the Naval and Military Wings of the Royal Flying Corps. The Naval Wing is concerned chiefly with airships, while the Military Wing is devoted to work with aeroplanes and man-carrying kites. The Corps has its foundation in the old Balloon Company of the Royal Engineers, which in 1911 was absorbed into the Air Battalion Royal Engineers, when the aerial service of the army was placed on a sound basis. The headquarters were placed at Aldershot. On April 13th, 1913, the Royal Flying Corps was organised and developed in remarkable manner in methods, material, and men. When war was declared against Germany in 1914 the members of the Corps quickly achieved fame by their efficiency and daring, many decorations being won, notably the V.C. by Lieut. Warneford, who was killed soon after in an accident near Paris.

Nicknames: "The Hawks," "The Sky Pilots."

"Dettingen," "Peninsula," "Waterloo," "Tel-el-Kebir," "Egypt, 1882," "Relief of Kimberley," "Paardeberg," "South Africa, 1899-1900."
Uniform, Scarlet.
Facings, Blue.
Cloak, Scarlet.
Head-dress, White metal helmet with white plume; band and trumpeters, scarlet plume.
Cap, Blue, with scarlet band.
On State occasions the band and trumpeters wear a special tunic of crimson heavily braided with gold.
A crimson cord is worn in the centre of the shoulder belt.
Two scarlet stripes are worn down the side seams of the overalls.
The Regiment carries three Squadron Standards in addition to the King's Standard. The Silver Kettle-Drums used in the Regiment were presented by King William IV in 1831.

1st LIFE GUARDS

In 1660, Charles II. before leaving Holland, formed into a troop a body of cavalier gentlemen who had rallied round him there, which he placed under the command of Lord Gerard. It was thus the Life Guards originated. The corps was styled "His Majesty's Own Troop of Guards."

The Life Guards were nicknamed "Cheeses," from the old gentlemen of the corps declining to serve in it as remodelled in 1788, saying "that it was no longer composed of gentlemen but of cheesemongers." Also known as "The Tin Bellies."

NOTE "A."—In full dress N.C.O.'s of the Household Cavalry do not wear chevrons but aiguillettes. The titles of the ranks also differ from other regiments—Corporal-Major (Sergeant-Major), Quartermaster-Corporal-Major (Quartermaster-Sergeant), Squadron-Corporal-Major (Squadron-Sergeant-Major), Corporal of Horse (Sergeant), Corporal (Corporal), Trooper (Private). The Farrier-Corporals carry polished pole axes on ceremonial parades, and wear black plumes and blue tunics.

"Dettingen," "Peninsula," "Waterloo," "Tel-el-Kebir," "Egypt, 1882," "Relief of Kimberley," "Paardeberg," "South Africa, 1899-1900."
Uniform, Scarlet.

Facings, Blue.
Cloak, Scarlet.
Head-dress, White metal helmet with white plume; band and trumpeters, scarlet plume.
Cap, Blue, with scarlet band.

On State occasions the band and trumpeters wear a special tunic of crimson heavily braided with gold.

A blue cord is worn in the centre of the shoulder belt.

Two scarlet stripes are worn down the side seams of the overalls.

The Regiment carries three Squadron Standards in addition to the King's Standard.

The Silver Kettle-Drums used in the Regiment were presented by King William IV, in 1831.

2nd LIFE GUARDS

This Corps formed by Charles II was styled in 1660 "The Duke of Albemarle's Troop of Guards," in 1670 "The Queen's Troop of Life Guards," and not till 1788 the 2nd Life Guards. Life Guards were at one time known as "Cheeses," from the old gentlemen of the corps declining to serve in it as remodelled in 1788, saying "that it was no longer composed of gentlemen but of cheesemongers." The name fell into desuetude, but was revived at the battle of Waterloo, when the officer in command shouted "Come on, Cheesemongers, charge!" Also known as "The Tin Bellies" (from the cuirasses).

See Note "A," 1st Life Guards.

"Dettingen," "Warburg," "Beaumont," "Willems," "Peninsula," "Waterloo," "Tel-el-Kebir," "Egypt, 1882," "Relief of Kimberley," "Paardeberg," "South Africa, 1899-1900."

Uniform, Blue.
Facings, Scarlet.
Cloak, Blue.
Head-dress, White metal helmet with red plume.

On State occasions the band and trumpeters wear a special tunic of crimson heavily braided with gold.

A crimson cord it worn in the centre of the shoulder belt.

A broad scarlet stripe is worn down the sides of the overalls.

In addition to the four Standards carried by the Household Cavalry, the Royal Horse Guards have a crimson silk Standard presented by King William IV.

The Silver Kettle Drums were presented by King George III.

ROYAL HORSE GUARDS (The Blues)

The Royal Horse Guards is the only cavalry regiment now in existence that formed part of the Parliamentary Army during the reign of Charles I. In the autumn of 1660, after the Restoration, its disbandment was ordered but not carried out, and King Charles "gave orders for raising a regiment of horse of eight troops, of which the Earl of Oxforde was to be Collonel, and also of a troop of horse guards." This was done under a Royal Warrant of 26th of January, 1661. In 1690 the regiment was called "The Oxford Blues" to distinguish it from the Earl of Portland's (Dutch) "Horse Guards." During the campaign in Flanders (1742-1745) it was known as "The Blue Guards," and is now popularly called "The Blues."

See Note "A," 1st Life Guards.

The Standard and Uniforms of the 3rd Dragoon Guards
The Drum Horse of the 7th Dragoon Guards—Review Order

(*Depot*, Dunbar.)

On Standard, The Royal Cypher within the Garter.

"Blenheim," "Ramillies," "Oudenarde," "Malplaquet," "Dettingen," "Warburg," "Beaumont," "Waterloo," "Sevastopol," "Taku Forts," "Pekin, 1860," "South Africa, 1879, 1901-02."

Uniform, Scarlet.

Facings, Blue.

Head-dress, Brass helmet with red plume; band, white plume.

Forage cap, Blue, with blue band.

Linked Regiment, 5th Dragoon Guards.

The Sergeants are entitled to wear the Regimental badge on their chevrons.

1st (King's) DRAGOON GUARDS

The 1st Dragoon Guards were styled "The Queen's Regiment of Horse" when first raised in 1685 on the accession of James II. When in Flanders with Marlborough, the regiment wore cuirasses, and had bright yellow facings. In 1714, in recognition of its brilliant services, the title was changed to "The King's Regiment of Horse," and in 1746 to "The 1st (or King's) Regiment of Dragoon Guards." A detachment of the regiment captured the Zulu King Cetewayo after his defeat at the battle of Ulundi. The battlefields of Flanders figure in the regiment's history no less than four times, viz.: In 1695 under King William at the siege of Namur; in 1704-9 under Marlborough at

Schellenberg, Blenheim, Ramillies, Oudenarde, and Malplaquet; in 1759 when it fought at Minden and elsewhere; and in the Great War, 1914.

Nicknames: "The K.D.G.'s," also "The Trades Union."

(*Depot*, Newport, Mon.)
On Standard, the Cypher of Queen Caroline within the Garter.
"Warburg," "Willems," "Lucknow," "South Africa, 1901-02."
Motto: "*Pro Rege et Patria*" (For King and for Country).
Uniform, Scarlet.
Facings, Buff.
Head-dress, Brass helmets with black plume; band, white plume.
Forage cap, Blue with buff band.
Linked Regiment, 6th (Inniskilling) Dragoons.
Special arm badge for Sergeants: "Bays" within a laurel wreath surmounted by a crown.

2nd DRAGOON GUARDS (Queen's Bays)

The 2nd Dragoon Guards was raised in 1685, and in 1687 called "The 3rd Horse," then "The Princess of Wales's Own Royal Regiment of Horse," in 1727 "The Queen's Own Royal Regiment of Horse," in 1746 "The 2nd Queen's Bays, or 2nd Regiment of Dragoon Guards," and in 1767 its present title of "Queen's Bays," from the circumstances of the corps being entirely mounted on bay chargers, the other heavy regiments (except the Scots Greys) having black horses. The regiment was much distinguished for its gallantry at the battle of Almanza, and in Flanders under King William.

Nicknames: At one time known as the "Rusty Buckles," and more popularly as "The Bays."

(*Depot*, Newport, Mon.)
On Standard, The Plume of the Prince of Wales. The Rising Sun in second corner, and the Red Dragon of Cadwaller in the third corner.
"Blenheim," "Ramillies," "Oudenarde," "Malplaquet," "Warburg," "Beaumont," "Willems," "Talavera," "Albuhera," "Vittoria," "Peninsula," "Abyssinia," "South Africa, 1901-02."
Uniform, Scarlet.
Facings, Yellow.
Head-dress, Brass helmet with black and red plume; band, red and white plume.

Forage cap, Blue with yellow band.
Linked Regiment, 6th Dragoon Guards (Carabiniers).
Special arm badge for Sergeants, Prince of Wales's Plume.

3rd (Prince of Wales's) DRAGOON GUARDS

The 3rd Dragoon Guards, originally "Cuirassiers," was raised in 1685, and after the battle of Sedgemoor its six troops were incorporated into a regiment called "The 4th Horse." In 1746 it was named "The 3rd Regiment of Dragoon Guards," and in 1765 "The Prince of Wales's Regiment of Dragoon Guards." At Ramillies it captured the standard and kettledrums of the Bavarian Guards. It was the only British Cavalry Regiment to take part in the Abyssinian campaign under Gen. Napier and formed part of the British column that made the memorable march on Magdala.

Nicknamed the "Old Canaries," on account of its facings being yellow, or canary colour.

(*Depot*, Newport, Mon.)
On Standard, the Harp and Crown and the Star of the Order of St. Patrick.
"Peninsula," "Balaklava," "Sevastopol," "Tel-el-Kebir," "Egypt, 1882."
Motto: *Quis separabit?* (Who shall separate?)
Uniform, Scarlet.
Facings, Blue.
Head-dress, Brass helmet with white plume; band, black plume.
Forage cap, Blue, with blue band.
Linked Regiment, 7th Dragoon Guards.
Special arm badge for Sergeants, Star of the Order of St. Patrick.

4th (Royal Irish) DRAGOON GUARDS

The 4th Dragoon Guards raised in 1685, was originally known as "Arran's Cuirassiers," or the "6th Horse," and in 1788 "The Fourth Dragoon Guards," and later on the words "Royal Irish" were added. Whilst on service in Ireland it obtained the name of the "Blue Horse," from its facings being of that colour. During the Crimean War the regiment took part in the famous charge of the Heavy Brigade at Balaklava, a memorable feat which has hardly received the recognition it deserved. The regiment rode into the charge cheering madly and did terrible execution. They are the only regiment of Dragoon Guards with an Irish title.

Nicknames: "The Buttermilks" on account of their lengthened stay in Ireland, during which many of the men acquired farms; and the "Mounted Micks."

(*Depot*, Dunbar).

On Standard, the Regimental device within a union wreath.

"Blenheim," "Ramillies," "Oudenarde," "Malplaquet," "Beaumont," "Salamanca," "Vittoria," "Toulouse," "Peninsula," "Balaklava," "Sevastopol," "Defence of Ladysmith," "South Africa, 1899-1902."

Motto: "*Vestigia nulla retrorsum*" (No going backward).

Uniform, Scarlet.

Facings, Dark Green.

Head-dress, Brass helmet with red and white plume; band, red plume.

Forage cap, Blue, with dark green band.

Linked Regiment, 1st (King's) Dragoon Guards.

Special arm badge for Sergeants, White Horse of Hanover.

At Salamanca it captured the staff of the drum-major of the French 66th Regiment. This is still carried on special parades by the trumpet-major.

5th (Princess Charlotte of Wales's) DRAGOON GUARDS

The 5th Dragoon Guards was raised in 1685, and was then the "Seventh Horse." During Marlborough's campaigns it won fame on many fields. Led by General Cadogan in person they rode down the Bavarian Horse Grenadier Guards, and drove them through the French infantry in rear, capturing many standards. Its present full title, was given it in 1804, after the Irish rebellion of 1798. During this latter period it was familiarly known as the "Green Horse," from its facings, and the "Green Dragoon Guards." During the Crimean War the regiment took part at Balaklava in the famous charge of the Heavy Brigade, led by their Colonel, Yorke-Scarlett.

Nicknames: "The Old Farmers" on account of their lengthened stay in Ireland, and the "Green Horse."

(*Depot*, Newport, Mon.)

"Blenheim," "Ramillies," "Oudenarde," "Malplaquet," "Warburg," "Willems," "Sevastopol," "Delhi, 1857," "Afghanistan, 1879-80," "Relief of Kimberley," "Paardeberg," "South Africa, 1899-1902."

Uniform, Blue.

Facings, White.

Head-dress, Brass helmet with white plume; band, red plume.

Forage cap, Blue with white band.

In 1851 the colour of the tunic was changed from scarlet to blue.

Linked Regiment, 3rd (Prince of Wales's) Dragoon Guards.

Allied Regiments, 1st and 2nd Mounted Rifles (Natal Carabineers of South Africa).

6th DRAGOON GUARDS (Carabiniers)

The 6th Dragoon Guards raised in 1685 as the "Queen Dowager's Regiment of Horse" and became the "Queen Dowager's Cuirassiers."

William III gave the regiment its name of King's Carabiniers in 1691 as a title of honour in recognition of its distinguished services. The name is also derived from the fact that the men were armed with long pistols called "Carabines." Many regiments on the Continent at this time were called Carabiniers. Its present name was given it in 1788. It greatly distinguished itself during Marlborough's campaigns, taking part in sieges and minor affairs without number. It was at Meerut on the outbreak of the Indian Mutiny and rendered the most valuable service throughout the campaign. The regiment has a very brilliant record of service.

Nicknames: "Tichborne's Own," since the trial of Arthur Orton, Sir Roger Tichborne having served in the regiment; and "The Carbs."

(*Depot*, Newport, Mon.)

On Standard, in the centre, the Coronet of Princess Royal.

"Blenheim," "Ramillies," "Oudenarde," "Malplaquet," "Dettingen," "Warburg," "South Africa, 1846-7," "Tel-el-Kebir," "Egypt, 1882," "South Africa, 1900-02."

Motto: *Quo fata vocant* (Where Fate calls).

Uniform, Scarlet.

Facings, Black.

Head-dress, Brass helmet, with black and white plume; band, white plume.

Forage cap, Blue, with black band.

Linked Regiment, 4th (Royal Irish) Dragoon Guards.

Special arm badge for Sergeants, Ligonier's Crest.

7th (Princess Royal's) DRAGOON GUARDS

The 7th Dragoon Guards was raised in 1688 by the Earl of Devonshire, whose title it bore till 1690, when from its Colonel's name it was called "Schomberg's Horse"; in 1742 "Ligonier's Horse," and then "The Black Horse," and became celebrated as a model for efficiency and discipline. In 1788 the present title, "The 7th (Princess Royal's) Dragoon Guards," was given to it at Dettingen. The 7th captured from the enemy a pair of kettledrums, which are now in the Officers' Mess. A Standard carried at the battle of Dettingen was presented by King George II to Cornet Richardson who bore it. He had received upwards of thirty wounds, but he refused to surrender, and preserved the Standard which is still in the possession of his descendants. Nicknames: In the reign of George II, "The Virgin Mary's Body Guard," having been sent to assist the army of the Archduchess Mary Theresa of Austria, also "Strawboots," because the men wrapped straw round their legs in a wet campaign; popularly known as "The Black Horse."

(*Depot*, Dunbar.)
On Guidon, The Crest of England within the Garter.
"Tangier, 1662-80," "Dettingen," "Warburg," "Beaumont," "Willems," "Fuentes d'Onor," "Peninsula," "Waterloo," "Balaklava," "Sevastopol," "Relief of Ladysmith," "South Africa, 1899-1902."
Motto: *Spectemur Agendo* (Let us be judged by our deeds).
Uniform, Scarlet.
Facings, Blue.
Head-dress, White metal helmet with black plume; band, white plume.
Forage cap, Blue, with scarlet band.
Linked Regiment, 2nd Dragoons (Royal Scots Greys).
Special arm badge for Sergeants, the Royal Crest.

1st (Royal) DRAGOONS

The Royals originated in a troop of Cuirassiers formed in 1661, on the marriage of Charles II with the Infanta Catherine of Portugal, and which was sent to garrison Tangier, whence they got the name of "Tangier Cuirassiers." In 1684 it was styled "The Royal Regiment of Dragoons," and each troop was furnished with a crimson Standard with badges embroidered upon them of (1) The King, (2) The Black Prince, (3) Henry V, (4) Henry VI, (5) Henry VII (Queen Mary I), (6) Queen Elizabeth. Towards the close of the 17th Century it was known as the "English Horse." At the battle of Dettingen it captured the white Standard of the French Mousquetaires Noirs. Its gallantry at the battle of Waterloo, where it formed part of the Union Brigade, is a matter of history.

Nicknames: "The Birdcatchers," for the capture of a French Eagle at the battle of Waterloo, and "The Royals."

Grenadier Guards.—Sergeant-Drummer in State Dress.
Sergeant Ewart capturing the Eagle at Waterloo.

(*Depot*, Dunbar.)
On Guidon, the Thistle within the Circle and Motto of the Order of the Thistle.
"Blenheim," "Ramillies," "Oudenarde," "Malplaquet," "Dettingen," "Warburg,"

"Willems," "Waterloo," "Balaklava," "Sevastopol," "Relief of Kimberley," "Paardeberg," "South Africa, 1899-1902."

Motto: Second to None.

Uniform, Scarlet.

Facings, Blue.

Head-dress, Bearskin cap, with a silver badge of a white horse at the back; hackle or plume, white; band, scarlet hackle.

Forage cap, Blue, with white vandyked band.

Linked Regiment, 1st Royal Dragoons.

Special arm badge for Sergeants, an Eagle.

2nd DRAGOONS (Royal Scots Greys)

Raised in 1678. In 1700 the corps was known as "The Grey Dragoons," and "The Scots Regiment of White Horses." In 1707, "The Royal Regiment of North British Dragoons." In 1713, "The 2nd Dragoons." And in 1866, "The 2nd Royal North British Dragoons, Scots Greys." At Waterloo, the regiment with a shout of "Scotland for ever," charged the French infantry masses and almost annihilated them. In the charge the eagle of the 45th French Regiment was captured by Sergeant Ewart; at Ramillies (1706) the Scots Greys captured the colours of the French "Regiment du Roi" and for this it was permitted to wear grenadier or bearskin caps.

The men have the nicknames of "Bubbly Jocks," owing to their dress. "Bubbly Jock" being a Scottish name for a turkey cock; "The Birdcatchers," in commemoration of the capture of an Eagle at Waterloo; also "The Greys."

(*Depot*, Bristol.)

"Dettingen," "Salamanca," "Vittoria," "Toulouse," "Peninsula," "Cabool, 1842," "Moodkee," "Ferozeshah," "Sobraon," "Chillianwallah," "Goojerat," "Punjaub," "South Africa, 1902."

Motto: Nec aspera terrent (Nor do difficulties deter).

Uniform, Blue.

Collar, Scarlet.

Head-dress, Busby with white plume and garter-blue busby bag.

Horse plume, White. Leopard skin saddlecloth.

Forage cap, Red.

Linked Regiment, 7th (Queen's Own) Hussars.

Special arm badge for Sergeants, White Horse of Hanover.

The regiment has an additional sergeant as kettle-drummer who, on ceremonial occasions, wears a silver collar which was presented by the wife of the Hon. Charles Fitzroy, afterwards Lord Southampton, on his being appointed colonel in 1772.

3rd (King's Own) HUSSARS

The 3rd Hussars, raised in 1685, was styled the "Queen Consort's Regiment of Dragoons." On the accession of George I it was called the "King's Own Dragoons." In 1861 the regiment became "Hussars." It was nicknamed "Lord Adam Gordon's Life Guards," from that officer detaining it for such a long period in Scotland when he commanded there.

It was also known as "Bland's Dragoons." At Dettingen the regiment lost very heavily, and in the following year it was reviewed by the King, who remarked with some asperity on its attenuated appearance, and inquired whose regiment it was, and where were the rest of the men. "The regiment is mine, your Majesty," replied the gallant Col. Bland, "and I believe the rest are at Dettingen."

(*Depot*, Dublin.)

"Dettingen," "Talavera," "Albuhera," "Salamanca," "Vittoria," "Toulouse," "Peninsula," "Ghuznee, 1839," "Affghanistan, 1839," "Alma," "Balaklava," "Inkerman," "Sevastopol."

Motto: *Mente et Manu* (With heart and hand).
Uniform, Blue.
Head-dress, Busby with scarlet plume and yellow busby bag.
Forage cap, Red.
Horse plume, Scarlet.
Linked Regiment, 8th (King's Royal Irish) Hussars.

4th (Queen's Own) HUSSARS

Originally raised in 1685 under the name of "The Princess Anne of Denmark's Regiment of Dragoons," became the 4th (Queen's Own) Hussars in 1861. As heavy cavalry the regiment fought in the Peninsular War, some brilliant exploits were performed. In 1818 the regiment became Light Dragoons, and the Regiment wore scarlet uniform with straw coloured facings, the uniform afterwards being changed back to light green. During the Crimean War it took part in the famous charge of the Light Brigade, under its Colonel, Lord George Paget, who led them with a cry of "Tally ho!" as they charged the enemy's guns. When the regiment formed part of the "Army of the Indus" under Lord Keane it was nicknamed "Paget's Irregular Horse," in consequence of its loose drill, the result of long service in the field.

(*Depot*, Woolwich.)
"Blenheim," "Ramillies," "Oudenarde," "Malplaquet," "Suakin, 1885," "Defence of Ladysmith," "South Africa, 1899-1902."
Motto: *Quis separabit?* (Who shall separate?)
Uniform, Blue.
Facings, Scarlet.
Head-dress, Lance cap of black leather with upper part and top of scarlet cloth. Green plume.
Forage cap, Blue, with scarlet band.
Linked Regiment, 12th (Prince of Wales's Royal) Lancers.
Special arm badge for Sergeants, Harp and Crown.

5th (Royal Irish) LANCERS

Raised as the "Royal Irish Dragoons" in 1689, and in 1858 became "The 5th (Royal Irish) Lancers." In recognition of the prominent part it took in Marlborough's campaigns, and particularly of its distinguished conduct at Blenheim, Marlborough directed that the captured kettledrums should be borne at the head of the regiment, and that the establishment should be nine troops. At Ramillies, with the Royal Scots Greys, it cut off two battalions of the Grenadiers of Picardie, and almost annihilated a third battalion before a body of French horse galloped to the rescue. To this the regiment owed the privilege it formerly enjoyed of wearing Grenadier caps like the Royal Scots Greys.

Nicknames: At one time called "The Daily Advertisers." More popularly known as "The Redbreasts" or "Irish Lancers."

The Coldstreamers first meeting with the Monarch.
Scots Guards—Piper in State Dress.

(*Depot*, Newport, Mon.)
On Guidon, The Castle of Inniskilling, with the St. George's Colours, and the word "Inniskilling" underneath.
"Dettingen," "Warburg," "Willems," "Waterloo," "Balaklava," "Sevastopol," "South Africa, 1899-1902."
Uniform, Scarlet.
Facings, Primrose.
Head-dress, White metal helmet, with white plume; band, scarlet plume.
Forage cap, Blue, with primrose band.
Horse plume, White.

Linked Regiment, 2nd Dragoon Guards (Queen's Bays).
Allied Regiment, 25th Brant Dragoons of Canada, Brantford, Ontario.
Special arm badge for Sergeants, Castle of Inniskilling.

6th (Inniskilling) DRAGOONS

The regiment was raised in 1689. In 1690 the corps was styled the "6th, or The Inniskilling Regiment of Dragoons." Its brilliant conduct as part of the Union Brigade at the Battle of Waterloo is a matter of history. During the Crimean War it took part in the famous charge of the Heavy Brigade at Balaklava, a memorable feat which has hardly received the recognition it deserved. Of more recent years the regiment saw a great deal of active service in South Africa.

About 1715 it was known as "The Black Dragoons," from being mounted on black horses. It achieved a high reputation for gallantry in Flanders.

Nicknames: "The old Inniskillings," and "The Skillingers." Popularly known as "The Inniskillings," from its badge "The Castle of Inniskilling."

(*Depot*, Bristol.)
"Dettingen," "Warburg," "Beaumont," "Willems," "Orthes," "Peninsula," "Waterloo," "Lucknow," "South Africa, 1901-02."
Uniform, Blue.
Head-dress, Busby with white plume, and scarlet busby bag.
Forage cap, Red.
Horse plume, White. Leopard skin saddlecloth.
Collar badge, the letters "Q.O." interlaced, within the Garter.
Linked Regiment, 3rd (King's Own) Hussars.

The only cavalry regiment in which the Officers are permitted to wear white strip collars with the frock coat.

7th (Queen's Own) HUSSARS

The regiment was raised in 1689 and called "Cunningham's Regiment of Dragoons." It was, during the Peninsular War, jocularly nicknamed "The Old Saucy Seventh," also "The Lily White Seventh," from its pale blue uniform and white facings, and also "Young Eyes." It was at first a Scotch Regiment, and it is the custom of its band to play "The Garb of old Gaul" when marching past, and "Hieland Laddie" when trotting. Also called the "Black Horse." It was the senior of the Light Dragoon Regiments when first connected with Hussars. It distinguished itself during the Indian Mutiny, particularly at the passage of the Betwa, where it had a hand-to-hand fight with the enemy's cavalry in the bed of the river. The name of the "Old Straws," or "Strawboots," originated at Warburg, 1760. The boots of the troopers being worn out, straw-bands were substituted for them.

(*Depot*, Dublin.)
"Leswarree," "Hindoostan," "Alma," "Balaklava," "Inkerman," "Sevastopol," "Central India," "Afghanistan, 1879-80," "South Africa, 1900-02."
Motto: "*Pristinæ virtutis memores*" (The memory of former valour).
Uniform, Blue.
Collar badge, The Harp and Crown.
Head-dress, Busby, with red and white plume and scarlet busby bag.
Forage cap, Red.
Linked Regiment, 4th (Queen's Own) Hussars.
Special arm badge for Sergeants, Harp and Crown.

8th (King's Royal Irish) HUSSARS

The 8th Hussars was raised in Ireland in 1693 and has always been closely associated with the Emerald Isle. It was known as "St. George's" from its Colonel's name in 1740-55; also as the "Cross Belts" in 1768 from the circumstance that it was permitted to wear the sword belt over the right shoulder, in place of round the waist as usual in dragoon regiments, for its gallant conduct at the battle of Saragossa, where it captured the belts of the Spanish cavalry. The regimental motto "*Pristinæ virtutis memores*," was specially conferred on their corps in commemoration of its brilliant gallantry at the battle of Leswarree in India. During the Crimean War it formed one of the regiments in the famous charge of the Light Brigade at the battle of Balaklava. The 8th Hussars and 17th Lancers have seen much service together, and they call themselves from their numbers "The Twenty Fives."

In the Indian Mutiny five Victoria Crosses were won by the regiment.

(*Depot*, Woolwich.)
"Peninsula," "Punniar," "Sobraon," "Chillianwallah," "Goojerat," "Punjaub," "Delhi, 1857," "Lucknow," "Charasiah," "Kabul, 1879," "Kandahar, 1880," "Afghanistan, 1878-80," "Modder River," "Relief of Kimberley," "Paardeberg," "South Africa, 1899-1902."
Uniform, Blue.
Facings, Scarlet.
Head-dress, Lance cap of black leather, with the upper part and top of blue cloth; black and white plume.

Forage cap, Blue, with scarlet band.
Linked Regiment, 21st (Empress of India's) Lancers.
Special arm badge for Sergeants, Queen Adelaide's Cypher and Crown.
The Officers wear a gold instead of a silver pouch.

9th (Queen's Royal) LANCERS

The regiment was originally raised in 1697, and re-embodied in 1715. They were known as "Wynne's Dragoons," and received their title in 1830 in honour of Queen Adelaide. Soon after its formation the regiment served continuously in Ireland for 86 years. It has seen much service in India. It particularly distinguished itself in the first Sikh War at Sobraon, and in the second Sikh War at Chillianwallah and Goojerat. At the siege of Delhi the natives called them "The Delhi Spearmen," from the good use they made of their long lances against the rebels. During the Afghan War it took part in Lord Roberts's march to Kandahar. At one period in its history the troopers wore crimson overalls.

Irish Guards.—The Officer of the Guard.
Welsh Guards.—Ceremonial Duty.

(*Depot*, Scarborough.)
"Warburg," "Peninsula," "Waterloo," "Sevastopol," "Ali Masjid," "Afghanistan, 1878-79," "Egypt, 1884," "Relief of Kimberley," "Paardeberg," "South Africa, 1899-1902."
Uniform, Blue.
Head-dress, Busby with black and white plume and scarlet busby-bag.
Forage cap, Red.
Linked Regiment, 18th (Queen Mary's Own) Hussars.
In Levee Dress the officers wear pantaloons of scarlet cloth.
Special arm badge for Sergeants, Prince of Wales's Plume.
In Review Order the saddlery of the officers' chargers is ornamented with cowrie shells.

10th (Prince of Wales's Own Royal) HUSSARS

Originally raised in 1697, and in 1783, was known as the "Prince of Wales's Light Dragoons." In 1793 the Prince of Wales (afterwards George IV) was appointed "Commandant," and in 1796 "Colonel" of the regiment. In 1811 the title "Royal" was conferred on it.
The regiment performed good service during the Peninsular War, and at Waterloo. It

was one of the regiments summoned from India during the Crimean War. Dressed in plain clothes, the officers and men were sent up the Red Sea and taken across the desert to Alexandria, thence to the seat of war.

Nicknames: "Baker's Light Bobs;" "The Chainy 10th," from the pattern of the pouch belt.

(*Depot*, Dublin.)
The Sphinx superscribed "Egypt."
"Warburg," "Beaumont," "Willems," "Salamanca," "Peninsula," "Waterloo," "Bhurtpore," "Alma," "Balaklava," "Inkerman," "Sevastopol."
Motto: "*Treu und Fest*" (True and Steadfast).
Uniform, Blue.
Overalls, Crimson.
Head-dress, Busby with crimson and white plume, and crimson busby bag. Band, grey fur busbies.
Horse plume, Black and white.
Forage cap, Crimson.
Linked Regiment, 13th Hussars.
Special arm badge for Sergeants, Crest and Motto of the late Prince Consort.

11th (Prince Albert's Own) HUSSARS

Raised in 1697, and afterwards disbanded. Raised again in 1715 and later received the title of the "Prince Albert's Own," because it formed Prince Albert's escort, from Dover to Canterbury, on his arrival in England in 1840, to be married to Queen Victoria. The regiment was present at the Alma and at Inkerman, and was one of the five regiments which, under the leadership of Lord Cardigan, its former Colonel, rode "into the jaws of death," at Balaklava. One of the regiment, Trooper Hope, also rode in the charge of the Heavy Brigade on the same occasion. He did so without permission and started without arms.

Nicknames: "The Cherry Pickers," also "The Cherubims," from its crimson overalls, being the only regiment in the British Army entitled to wear overalls of that colour. Also known as "Lord Cardigan's Bloodhounds."

(*Depot*, Woolwich.)
The Sphinx superscribed "Egypt."
"Peninsula," "Waterloo," "South Africa, 1851-2-3." "Sevastopol," "Central India," "Relief of Kimberley," "Paardeberg," "South Africa, 1899-1902."

Uniform, Blue.
Facings, Scarlet.
Head-dress, Lance Cap, black leather, with upper part and top of scarlet cloth; scarlet plume.
Forage cap, Scarlet.
Allied Regiment, 12th Manitoba Dragoons of Canada.
Linked Regiment, 5th (Royal Irish) Lancers.
Special arm badge for Sergeants, Prince of Wales's Plume.
It has been the custom in this regiment for the band to play five hymns every evening at tattoo. One version of the legend is that it was a punishment for breaking into a monastery during the Peninsular War, the punishment to last a hundred years. Another version is that these hymns were presented to the officers by Pope Pius VI for the band to play. Whoever originated the custom we can all sympathise with the unfortunate bandsmen who have to carry out the bequest.

12th (Prince of Wales's Royal) LANCERS

The regiment was raised in 1715, and served uninterruptedly in Ireland for 76 years. It won high reputation during the Peninsular War. It subsequently fought gallantly at Quatre Bras and at Waterloo. It was one of the regiments summoned from India to the Crimea, proceeding there by way of the Red Sea and across the desert to Alexandria. It subsequently returned to India and bore a distinguished part in the operations in Central India under Sir Hugh Rose during the Mutiny.

Nicknamed the "Supple Twelfth" at Salamanca, from its dash and rapidity of movement, in action.

(*Depot*, Dublin.)
"Albuhera," "Vittoria," "Orthes," "Toulouse," "Peninsula," "Waterloo," "Alma," "Balaklava," "Inkerman," "Sevastopol," "Relief of Ladysmith," "South Africa, 1899-1902."
Motto: *Viret in Æternum* (It flourishes for ever).
Uniform, Blue.
Collars, Buff.
Head-dress, Busby, with white plume and buff busby bag.
Forage cap, White, with blue band.
Horse plume, White.
Linked Regiment, 11th (Prince Albert's Own) Hussars.
The "Honours" are worn on the Officers' shoulder belt.

13th HUSSARS

Raised in 1715 as "Munden's Dragoons"; was known as the "Green Dragoons" from its facings; and in the Peninsular War nicknamed the "Ragged Brigade" for its inability to keep a trim appearance owing to its hard and severe work during 32 actions, in which it lost 276 men and over 1,000 horses. It fought gallantly at Waterloo. It was present throughout the Crimean War, and was engaged at the Alma and at Inkerman. It was one of the regiments of the Light Brigade in the famous Balaklava charge, and afterwards served before Sevastopol.

Known as "The Lilywhites," on account of its white collars on tunics and white stripes down overalls. Also known as "The Evergreens," from the old green facings and motto; and "The Geraniums," from the smart dress of the officers and men.

(*Depot*, Scarborough.)
The Royal Crest within the Garter.
"Douro," "Talavera," "Fuentes d'Onor," "Salamanca," "Vittoria," "Pyrenees," "Orthes," "Peninsula," "Punjaub," "Chillianwallah," "Goojerat," "Persia," "Central India," "Relief of Ladysmith," "South Africa, 1900-02."
Uniform, Blue.
Head-dress, Busby, with white plume and yellow busby bag.
Forage cap, Red.
Linked Regiment, 20th Hussars.

14th (King's) HUSSARS

Originally raised in 1697 and disbanded. Again raised in 1715. It fought with distinction through the whole of the Peninsular War from first to last, and was engaged times without number. In the pursuit after the battle of Vittoria, the 14th came up with Joseph Buonaparte's carriage, from which he had but just escaped, leaving behind him a celebrated but indescribable silver trophy called The Emperor's Chambermaid, still widely renowned throughout the service. This is the corps of Charles O'Malley's choice, and mustered in its ranks the ever memorable Micky Free. In 1848 the regiment charged vastly superior numbers of the Sikh army at the battle of Ramnuggar, losing their Brigadier, their Colonel, and 40 officers and men, and have since been known as the Ramnuggar Boys—the anniversary of that battle being still observed as a great day in the regiment. It fought in Persia in 1857, and was particularly distinguished in Central India.

Nicknamed "The Emperor's Chambermaids."

(*Depot*, Bristol.)
The Crest of England within the Garter.
"Emsdorff," "Villers-en-Cauchies," "Willems," "Egmont-op-Zee," "Sahagun," "Vittoria," "Peninsula," "Waterloo," "Afghanistan, 1878-80."
Motto: *Merebimur* (We will deserve).
Uniform, Blue.
Head-dress, Busby with scarlet plume and busby bag.
Forage cap, Scarlet.
Horse plume, Scarlet.
Allied Regiment, 15th Light Horse of Canada, Calgary, Alberta.
Linked Regiment, 19th (Queen Alexandra's Own Royal) Hussars.
The officers wear crossed flags, pointing downwards, on the leopard skin.
Special arm badge for Sergeants, Royal Crest.

15th (The King's) HUSSARS

The 15th Hussars was the first regiment of Light Dragoons raised for permanent service in 1759 by Colonel Eliott, the gallant defender of Gibraltar, afterwards Lord Heathfield. It was named after him "Eliott's Light Horse." In 1767 the regiment was made "Royal" as a reward for its services in Germany, and in 1768 styled the "King's Light Dragoons." Its present title it received in 1806.

This regiment was authorized to bear on its helmets the following inscription: "Five battalions of Foot defeated and taken by this regiment, with their colours, and nine pieces of cannon, at Emsdorff, 16th July, 1760." In 1794, the 15th, at Villiers-en-Cauchies, charged enormously superior numbers of all arms. It succeeded in its object at a terrible sacrifice. In 1799, the troopers had given them the honour of decking their helmets with scarlet feathers.

Nicknamed "The Fighting Fifteenth."

(*Depot*, Woolwich.)
The Cypher of Queen Charlotte within the Garter.
"Beaumont," "Willems," "Talavera," "Fuentes d'Onor," "Salamanca," "Vittoria," "Nive," "Peninsula," "Waterloo," "Bhurtpore," "Ghuznee, 1839," "Affghanistan, 1839," "Maharajpore," "Aliwal," "Sobraon," "Relief of Kimberley," "Paardeberg," "South Africa, 1900-02."
Motto: *Aut cursu, aut cominus armis* (Either in the charge, or hand to hand).
Uniform, Scarlet.
Facings, Blue.

Head-dress, Lance cap of black leather with upper part and top of dark blue cloth; black plume.

Forage cap, Scarlet, with blue band.

Allied Regiment, 16th Light Horse of Canada, Regina, Saskatchewan.

Linked Regiment, 17th (Duke of Cambridge's Own) Lancers.

16th (The Queen's) LANCERS

The regiment was raised in 1759. It served with distinction throughout the Peninsular War, from Talavera to Toulouse, during the greater part of which time it was attached to the Light Division. Subsequently, it fought at Quatre Bras and at Waterloo, where it lost heavily. It was the first Lancer regiment to serve in India, and the first British Lancers to use the lance in action. During a tour of service in India extending over a quarter of a century it won great fame on many fields. At the battle of Aliwal (where Sir Harry Smith, with a force of 12,000 men with 32 guns, defeated 19,000 Sikhs with 68 guns) it specially distinguished itself.

The 16th Lancers, being the only Lancer corps wearing the scarlet tunic, received the sobriquet of the "Scarlet Lancers."

(*Depot*, Woolwich.)

Death's Head "*Or Glory.*"

"Alma," "Balaklava," "Inkerman," "Sevastopol," "Central India," "South Africa, 1879, 1900-02."

Uniform, Blue.

Facings, White.

Head-dress, Lance cap of black leather with white cloth top, white plume.

Forage cap, Blue, with white band.

Linked Regiment, 16th (The Queen's) Lancers.

Special arm badge for Sergeants, Death's Head.

17th (Duke of Cambridge's Own) LANCERS

The regiment was raised in 1759 and in 1876 received its present title of "17th (Duke of Cambridge's Own) Lancers." It was present throughout the Crimean War and fought at the Alma, Inkerman and Balaklava, where it was one of the five regiments that took part in the famous charge of the Light Brigade. It also fought in the Indian Mutiny.

Popularly known as the "Death or Glory Boys," and "Skull and Crossbones," from the circumstance that its Colonel (Hole) chose its crest of a "death's head" and its motto "*or glory*," as he wished all to remember General Wolfe, with whom he happened to serve in the year on which his regiment was first raised in Scotland by Lord Aberdour. Another nickname given them was that of "Bingham's Dandies," the uniform being of scarlet with white facings and overalls and black plume. The late Earl of Lucan, when Lord Bingham, was Lieutenant-Colonel of the corps, which was in his time remarkable for the well-fitting uniforms both of the officers and men belonging to it.

Charging with the Light Brigade at Balaclava.
Royal Engineers at Pontooning Work.

(*Depot*, Scarborough.)
"Peninsula," "Waterloo," "Defence of Ladysmith," "South Africa, 1899-1902."
Motto: *Pro Rege, pro Lege, pro Patria conamur* (We strive for King, for Law, for Country).
Uniform, Blue.
Head-dress, Busby with scarlet and white plume and blue busby bag.
Forage cap, Red.
Linked Regiment, 10th (Prince of Wales's Own Royal) Hussars.
Special arm badge for Sergeants, Q.M.O. Monogram.
The silver trumpets used by the regiment were provided out of proceeds of the sale of the captured horses at Waterloo.

18th (Queen Mary's Own) HUSSARS

Originally raised in 1759 by the Marquis of Drogheda, and disbanded in 1821, after brilliant service in the Peninsular War and at Waterloo. The regiment served in the Maroon War and at San Domingo, 1759-60, and lost so heavily from war and disease that it returned to England under the command of the regimental surgeon. At one time the Duke of Wellington served in the regiment, in command of a troop, before being transferred to the 33rd Foot as a field officer. The present regiment was raised at Leeds in 1858, and was permitted to revive the honours, "Peninsula" and "Waterloo," borne by the old regiment. It wore Lincoln green busby bags and plumes, and scarlet pouches and sabretaches. Its present title was conferred in 1910.

(*Depot*, Bristol.)
The Elephant, superscribed "Assaye."
"Mysore," "Seringapatam," "Niagara," "Tel-el-Kebir," "Egypt, 1882-84," "Abu Klea," "Nile, 1884-85," "Defence of Ladysmith," "South Africa, 1899-1902."
Uniform, Blue.
Head-dress, Busby with white plume and busby bag.

Forage cap, Red.
Horse plume, White.
Linked Regiment, 15th (The King's) Hussars.
Special arm badge for Sergeants, an Elephant.
Queen Alexandra's crest is used as a collar badge. In 1914 Her Majesty presented the regiment with a pair of beautiful kettle drum banners.

19th (Queen Alexandra's Own Royal) HUSSARS

Originally raised in 1759 as the 19th Light Dragoons, and converted into Hussars in 1807. The present regiment was formed in 1860 out of the late Hon. East India Company's Bengal European Cavalry. It was subsequently permitted to assume the honours of the old 19th Dragoons (Lancers): "Assaye" and "Niagara." It fought with distinction during the Egyptian War, 1882, Suakin, 1884, and in the Nile Expedition. Sir John French commenced his military career with the regiment.

Nicknamed the "Dumpies," from the circumstance of the men, originally taken over from the East India Company's 1st Bengal European Cavalry, being of diminutive size. The Indian history of the regiment is full of interest, for much hard service was seen and a good deal of heavy fighting, especially at Assaye, where, for its distinguished conduct, the badge of the Elephant was awarded.

(*Depot*, Scarborough.)
"Vimiera," "Peninsula," "Suakin, 1885," "South Africa, 1901-02."
Uniform, Blue.
Head-dress, Busby with yellow plume and crimson busby bag.
Horse plume, Yellow.
Forage cap, Red.
Linked Regiment, 14th (King's) Hussars.

20th HUSSARS

The Regiment was originally raised in Ireland in 1789 from the "Light Troop" of the 6th (Inniskilling) Dragoons, and wore a scarlet uniform, the facings being at first yellow and afterwards black. It is a curious fact that a detachment of the regiment under Sir Robert Wilson was present with the Russian Army in their operations against Napoleon in his famous capture of and return from Moscow in 1812 and in the subsequent campaign in Germany. The present regiment was raised in 1861 by volunteers from the late Hon. East India Company's 2nd Bengal European Light Cavalry. It was subsequently permitted to assume the honours of the old 20th Light

Dragoons: "Vimiera" and "Peninsula." Part of the regiment was employed in the Suakin Expedition, 1885, and subsequently did good service with the Egyptian Frontier Force in 1885-6.

Nicknamed the "X's."

(*Depot*, Woolwich.)
"Khartoum."
Uniform, Blue.
Facings, French grey.
Head-dress, Lance cap of black leather with upper part and top of french grey cloth, white plume.
Forage cap, Blue, with french grey band.
Linked Regiment, 9th (Queen's Royal) Lancers.
Special arm badge for Sergeants, Imperial Cypher and Crown.

21st (Empress of India's) LANCERS

Four British Cavalry regiments have in succession been numbered the 21st; the original regiment having been raised in 1760 as the 21st Light Dragoons, by the famous Marquis of Granby. It was disbanded in 1763, re-raised in 1779, and again disbanded. In 1794 it again appeared, and saw a great deal of service abroad, and served in St. Helena when Napoleon was imprisoned there. The uniform first was scarlet, and later blue, with pink facings, which was afterwards changed to black velvet.

Raised in 1858 as the 3rd Bengal European Cavalry. In 1862 it was transferred to the British establishment, and until 1897 was known as the 21st Hussars. In that year the title was changed to 21st Lancers, and in 1898, in recognition of its brilliant services at the battle of Omdurman, its present Royal title was conferred upon it.

Nickname: "The Grey Lancers."

Royal Field Artillery in Review Order—"Halt!"
The Heroic Stand of "L" Battery, R.H.A., at Nery, September 1st, 1914.

Mottoes: *Ubique* (Everywhere).*Quo Fas et Gloria ducunt* (Where Duty and Glory lead.)

Head-dress, Busby with white plume and scarlet busby bag. The R.A. Mounted Band wear scarlet plumes.
Forage cap, Blue with scarlet band.
Regimental March: "British Grenadiers."

The R.H.A. take precedence next the Household Cavalry, but when on parade with their guns take the right of the line.

ROYAL HORSE ARTILLERY

Although the Royal Regiment of Artillery dates back to the reign of King Henry VIII, the Horse Artillery was first organised in 1793. In 1794 the splendid service rendered by the Horse Batteries at Vaux led the Duke of York to direct it to march past the whole of the allied armies at a special parade. The famous Chestnut Troop (now "A" Battery) did equally good service in North Holland in 1799, and the famous Rocket Troop was raised for special service in Flanders. The Royal Horse Artillery have won fame on many hard fought battlefields, notably at Fuentes d'Onor, in the Peninsular War, where Norman Ramsay charged with his battery (now "I" Battery) through the enemy's cavalry; and in South Africa and France where "Q" Battery and "L" Battery won many Victoria Crosses.

Nicknames: "The Right of the Line," "The Galloping Gunners," and "The Four-wheeled Hussars."

Mottoes: *Ubique* (Everywhere). *Quo Fas et Gloria ducunt* (Where Duty and Glory lead).
Uniform, Blue.
Facings, Scarlet.
Girdle, Red and Blue.
Head-dress, Helmet with brass ball on top.
Forage cap, Blue with scarlet band.
Regimental March, "British Grenadiers."
Cap badge, A gun with motto.
Collar badge, A grenade.

ROYAL FIELD ARTILLERY

The Royal Regiment of Artillery, as it is now known, was formed in 1716, when two companies were permanently established at Woolwich, but, prior to that, artillery formed part of the King's Armies as early as the 15th century. The history of the Artillery is really the history of the British Army, for very seldom indeed has there been an action fought by British troops without some representatives of the Royal Regiment being present. The guns are looked upon as the standards of the regiment, and in the old days one of the guns was known as the colour gun, which was usually the heaviest piece in the field. All ranks are animated with the most intense bravery and devotion, which has been demonstrated on many fields, and won for the regiment many distinctions. The Great War on the Continent has added greatly to the reputation of the regiment.

Nicknamed "The Gunners."

Mottoes: *Ubique* (Everywhere).*Quo Fas et Gloria ducunt* (Where Duty and Glory lead).
Uniform, Blue.
Facings, Scarlet.
Belt, White.
Head-dress, Helmet with brass ball on top.
Forage cap, Blue with scarlet band.
Regimental March, "British Grenadiers."
Cap badge, A gun with motto.
Collar badge, A grenade.

ROYAL GARRISON ARTILLERY

The Garrison, or Heavy Gunners can be considered as the direct descendants of the ancient British Artillery, which was originally formed for siege or defence purposes. The more mobile Field and Horse Artillery was not formed till very many years later. The records of the Garrison Artillery show they have won glory in all parts of the world. The gallantry displayed during the two years defence of Gibraltar is among their most cherished traditions, and for distinguished conduct at the reduction of Martinique, No. 11 Company received as a mark of honour a battle axe, which was directed to be carried by the tallest gunner at the head of the battery when on parade. The splendid achievements of the Heavy Artillery in the great war with Germany has added materially to the reputation of the regiment for gallantry and valour.

Nicknamed the "Heavy Gunners."

Mottoes: *Ubique* (Everywhere).*Quo Fas et Gloria ducunt* (Where Duty and Glory lead).
Uniform, Scarlet.
Facings, Blue velvet.
Head-dress, Helmet with brass spike on top.
Forage cap, Blue.
Field Officers when attending Court or Levees wear the cocked hat.
Regimental March, "British Grenadiers."

The band wear a bearskin cap in full dress.

CORPS OF ROYAL ENGINEERS

The Corps can trace its history back as a distinct organization to 1717, but Engineers or artificers were known before that. In 1722 the Corps was known as "The Soldier Artificier Corps," and later as "The Corps of Military Artificers." In 1788, under Master-General the Duke of Richmond, the Officers were constituted "The Corps of Royal Engineers," the other ranks being "The Royal Line Artificers." The title of "The Royal Sappers and Miners" replaced them in 1813, and for their distinguished service in the Crimea all ranks were united under the title of "The Corps of Royal Engineers." Of the services, individual and collective, of the Corps during its history it would be impossible to treat in detail, for they have served with distinction in every battle and in all parts of the Empire, and have a glorious history of unusual valour.

Nicknames: "The Sappers"; "The Mudlarks"; "The Measurers"; and "The Mounted Bricklayers."

(*Regimental Headquarters*, Buckingham Gate, S.W.)

"Tangier, 1680," "Namur, 1695," "Gibraltar, 1704-5," "Blenheim," "Ramillies," "Oudenarde," "Malplaquet," "Dettingen," "Lincelles," "Egmont-op-Zee," "Corunna," "Barrosa," "Nive," "Peninsula," "Waterloo," "Alma," "Inkerman," "Sevastopol," "Tel-el-Kebir," "Egypt, 1882," "Suakin, 1885," "Khartoum," "Modder River," "South Africa, 1899-1902."

Uniform, Scarlet.

Facings, Blue.

Head-dress, Bearskin cap with white plume worn on left side.

Forage cap, Blue with scarlet band.

Regimental March, "British Grenadiers."

Buttons on the tunic are placed at equal distance apart.

GRENADIER GUARDS

The Grenadier Guards were raised in the year 1657, when the loyal English who shared King Charles's exile were formed into six regiments, the first of which was called the "Royal Regiment of Guards."

For the first seventy years of its existence it saw much and varied service, and won fame on many fields, and also served on board the fleet. During the Peninsular War its good order and steady discipline were conspicuous. Its conduct at Waterloo is a matter of history, and its heroic bearing during the Crimean War is well known.

The title of "Grenadiers" was given to the first Regiment of Foot Guards in 1815, in recognition of their having defeated the French Grenadier Guards at Waterloo.

The Grenadier Guards have the nicknames of the "Sand-bags," the "Coalheavers," and "Old Eyes," and the 3rd Battalion "The Bill Browns."

(*Regimental Headquarters*, Buckingham Gate, S.W.)

"Tangier, 1680," "Namur, 1695," "Gibraltar, 1704-5," "Oudenarde," "Malplaquet," "Dettingen," "Lincelles," "Talavera," "Barrosa," "Fuentes d'Onor," "Nive," "Peninsula," "Waterloo," "Alma," "Inkerman," "Sevastopol," "Tel-el-Kebir," "Egypt, 1882," "Suakin, 1885," "Modder River," "South Africa, 1899-1902."

Motto: Nulli Secundus (Second to none).

Uniform, Scarlet.

Facings, Blue.

Head-dress, Bearskin cap with red plume on right side.

Forage cap, Blue, with white band.

Regimental March, "Milanello."

Buttons on the Tunic are placed in twos.

COLDSTREAM GUARDS

The Coldstream Guards was originally formed from Sir A. Hesselrig's and Colonel Fenwick's Regiments of Foot, and obtained its title from Monck's celebrated march from Coldstream in January, 1660, to restore King Charles II. The regiment was also known as the "Nulli Secundus Club," and "The Coldstreamers." This is the only regiment of the Parliamentary Army that was not disbanded at the Restoration in 1660. Under Marlborough it shared in the great victories of Oudenarde and Malplaquet, and at many sieges and encounters down to the peace of 1713. It took part in most of the great battles of the Peninsular War. At Waterloo it was posted on the ridge above Hougoumont, and to it fell the honour of defending the Chateau of Hougoumont—the key of the British position—throughout that memorable day, and nobly was that duty performed. During the Crimean War the regiment fought splendidly, as it has on every subsequent occasion, and has worthily upheld its motto of *Nulli Secundus*.

(*Regimental Headquarters*: Buckingham Gate, S.W.)

"Namur, 1695," "Dettingen," "Lincelles," "Talavera," "Barrosa," "Fuentes d'Onor," "Nive," "Peninsula," "Waterloo," "Alma," "Inkerman," "Sevastopol," "Tel-el-Kebir," "Egypt, 1882," "Suakin, 1885," "Modder River," "South Africa, 1899-1902."

Motto: *Nemo me impune lacessit* (No one provokes me with impunity).

Uniform, Scarlet.
Facings, Blue.
Head-dress, Bearskin cap.
Forage cap, Blue, diced border.
Regimental March, "Highland Laddie."
Buttons on the tunic are placed in threes.

SCOTS GUARDS

The origin of this distinguished corps is uncertain, the regimental papers having been destroyed by fire in 1841; but it was raised about 1639, and was originally called by the same name it now bears, which, however, had been for a long time in disuse, and was only in 1877 restored to the corps by the late Queen Victoria. Previously it had been styled "The Scots Fusilier Guards" and the "3rd Foot Guards." Throughout its long career it has ever been distinguished for its valour and discipline. At Namur it advanced without firing a shot, but exposed to the murderous fire of the enemy from the ramparts, close up to the palisades, when they poured in their volleys and put the enemy to confusion. It distinguished itself at Lincelles for its coolness, steady fire and gallant bayonet charge. During the Peninsular War it was constantly engaged, and there and at subsequent battles not only upheld the traditions of the regiment, but gained a reputation no troops could surpass.

Nicknamed "The Jocks."

(*Regimental Headquarters*, Buckingham Gate, S.W.)
Motto: *Quis separabit?* (Who shall separate?)
Uniform, Scarlet.
Facings, Blue.
Head-dress, Bearskin cap with blue plume on right side.
Forage cap, Blue, with green band.
Regimental March, "St. Patrick's Day."
The Buttons on the Tunic are placed in fours.

IRISH GUARDS

Raised in 1900 by the late Queen Victoria to commemorate the bravery of the Irish Regiments in the South African War. All ranks have worthily upheld the high traditions of the Brigade of Guards in their first campaign, being distinguished for conspicuous bravery in many of the frequent actions against the overwhelming German forces in France and Belgium. Many decorations have been won, among them being the Victoria Cross awarded to Sergeant Michael O'Leary whose great bravery has been widely extolled among the Allies.

Nicknamed "Bob's Own," from the fact that the late Lord Roberts was the first Colonel of the regiment.

(*Regimental Headquarters*, Buckingham Gate, S.W.)
Motto: *Cymru am Byth* (Wales for Ever!)
Uniform, Scarlet.
Facings, Blue.
Head-dress, Bearskin cap with white, green, and white plume.
Badge, The Leek. The Red Dragon of Wales is emblazoned on the King's Colour.
Regimental March, "Men of Harlech."
Buttons on tunics are placed in sets of five.

WELSH GUARDS

This regiment was raised in London in 1915 by the Royal Warrant of King George V, during the progress of the War with Germany, and the first Battalion of 1,100 of all ranks, under Lieut.-Col. W. Murray Threipland, was quickly completed, a second Battalion being then authorised. Major-General Sir Francis Lloyd was the first Colonel of the regiment, and Col. Lord Harlech, who commenced his military career in the Coldstream Guards, was appointed to command the regiment and the regimental district. His Majesty in authorising the raising of the regiment directed that the leading company of the 1st Battalion should be denominated "The Prince of Wales's Company," in the same way as the leading company of the 1st Grenadier Guards is known as the "King's Company."

(*Depot*, Glencorse.)
(*Record Office*, Hamilton.)
The Sphinx, superscribed "Egypt."
"Tangier, 1680," "Namur, 1695," "Blenheim," "Ramillies," "Oudenarde," "Malplaquet," "Louisburg," "Havannah," "Egmont-op-Zee," "St. Lucia, 1803," "Corunna," "Busaco," "Salamanca," "Vittoria," "St. Sebastian," "Nive," "Niagara," "Peninsula," "Waterloo," "Nagpore," "Maheidpoor," "Ava," "Alma," "Inkerman," "Sevastopol," "Taku Forts," "Pekin, 1860," "South Africa, 1899-1902."
Motto: *Nemo me impune lacessit* (No one provokes me with impunity).
Uniform, Scarlet.
Facings, Blue.

Head-dress, Kilmarnock bonnet, with plume.
Cap, Glengarry, with scarlet, white and green diced border.
Regimental March, "Dumbarton's Drums."

Only the pipers wear the kilt of Royal Stewart tartan. The regiment wears the doublet, and trews of Hunting Stewart tartan.

THE ROYAL SCOTS

The Royal Scots have the proud distinction of being the oldest regiment in the British Army, dating its present existence from 1633. It was organised by Sir John Hepburn, and on his death 37 years later the command was given to Lord James Douglas and became known as "Douglas's Regiment." Nobly has it sustained its reputation, and in every quarter of the globe, the roll of "Dumbarton's Drums" has been heard.

"Pontius Pilate's Bodyguard" is the extraordinary nickname given to the regiment. This was on account of a dispute between the regiment (then the "Regiment de Douglas," or "Douglas Ecossais") when in the French service, and the Picardy Regiment, as to the antiquity of the two corps. The Picardy Regiment laid claim to having been on duty on the night after the Crucifixion. To this the 1st Foot wittily rejoined: "Had we been on duty, we should not have slept at our post."

(*Depot*, Guildford.)
(*Record Office*, Hounslow.)

A Naval Crown, superscribed "1st June, 1794." The Sphinx, superscribed "Egypt."
"Tangier, 1662-80," "Namur, 1695," "Vimiera," "Corunna," "Salamanca," "Vittoria," "Pyrenees," "Nivelle," "Toulouse," "Peninsula," "Ghuznee, 1839," "Khelat," "Affghanistan, 1839," "South Africa, 1851-2-3," "Taku Forts," "Pekin, 1860," "Burma, 1885-87," "Tirah," "Relief of Ladysmith," "South Africa, 1899-1902."

Mottoes: *Pristinæ virtutis memor* (Mindful of its ancient valour). *Vel exuviæ triumphant* (Even the remnant triumph).

Uniform, Scarlet.
Facings, Blue.
Head-dress, Helmet.
Cap, Blue, with scarlet band.
Regimental March, "We'll gang nae mair."

The Regiment has a third Colour, carried on State occasions.

THE QUEEN'S (Royal West Surrey Regiment)

The regiment is the oldest English infantry unit, having been raised in 1661 by the

Earl of Peterborough. Nicknamed "Kirke's Lambs," from its Colonel and badge in 1682. Was raised to garrison Tangier, and received then the badge of the "Paschal Lamb," the crest of the House of Braganza. Was known when raised as the "1st Tangerines." The title "Royal" and motto, *Pristinæ virtutis memor*, was conferred for its brilliant conduct at Tongres in 1685, where for 28 hours it gallantly maintained itself against 40,000 of the enemy, and by its heroism saved the rest of the army from being taken by surprise.

A detachment was on board the "Birkenhead" when that transport was wrecked, and in order to allow the women and children to be saved, stood firm in their ranks on the deck of the doomed ship, until the waves swallowed all but the deathless glory of their deed.

(*Depot*, Canterbury.)
(*Record Office*, Hounslow.)
"Blenheim," "Ramillies," "Oudenarde," "Malplaquet," "Dettingen," "Guadaloupe, 1759," "Douro," "Talavera," "Albuhera," "Vittoria," "Pyrenees," "Nivelle," "Nive," "Orthes," "Toulouse," "Peninsula," "Punniar," "Sevastopol," "Taku Forts," "South Africa, 1879," "Chitral," "Relief of Kimberley," "Paardeberg," "South Africa, 1900-02."
Motto: *Veteri frondescit honore* (May it flourish by its ancient honors).
Uniform, Scarlet.
Facings, Buff.
Head-dress, Helmet.
Cap, Blue.
Regimental March, "The Buffs."
Allied Regiment, 2nd Queen's Own Rifles of Canada, Toronto.

THE BUFFS (East Kent Regiment)

The 3rd Foot (The Buffs) was so called first in 1708. Its previous title was "The Holland Regiment," having been in the Dutch Service from the time of Queen Elizabeth. It was raised in 1572 to the number of 3000 men by London Guilds, when the Dutch were in revolt against Spain. To this circumstance, the regiment owes the time-honoured privilege it enjoys of marching through the City of London with drums beating and colours flying without let or hindrance, the custom being derived from the privileges of the Train Bands of Elizabethan days. It was nicknamed the "Buff Howards" from the colour of its facings and Colonel's name, 1737 to 1749; also the

"Old Buffs," to distinguish it from the 31st Regiment, which was the "Young Buffs." Other nicknames given were "The Nutcrackers," on account of its prowess in cracking the heads of the enemy, and "The Resurrectionists," which was obtained at Albuhera where the regiment was dispersed by the Polish Lancers, and reappeared shortly after.

(*Depot*, Lancaster.)
(*Record Office*, Preston.)
"Namur, 1695," "Gibraltar, 1704-5," "Guadaloupe, 1759," "St. Lucia, 1778," "Corunna," "Badajoz," "Salamanca," "Vittoria," "St. Sebastian," "Nive," "Peninsula," "Bladensburg," "Waterloo," "Alma," "Inkerman," "Sevastopol," "Abyssinia," "South Africa, 1879," "Relief of Ladysmith," "South Africa, 1899-1902."
Uniform, Scarlet.
Facings, Blue.
Head-dress, Helmet.
Cap, Blue with scarlet band.
Regimental March, "Corn rigs are bonnie."

THE KING'S OWN (Royal Lancaster Regiment)

The regiment was raised in 1680 by the Earl of Plymouth. It gained great distinction at the siege of Namur, 1695, and while serving as Marines in 1704 it shared in the capture of Gibraltar. It has fought with distinction in all parts of the world, and has ever acquitted itself with credit to England and glory to itself. It was one of the few British regiments to make the famous desert march across Abyssinia, to the capture of Magdala. It also fought in the Zulu War and was one of the devoted battalions to climb and capture Spion Kop, holding that awful position throughout a day of dire disaster with unflinching courage.

Nicknames: The "Lions," from its ancient badge, the Lion of England, given to it by the Prince of Orange, the regiment being the first to join his Standard after landing at Torbay in 1688. "Barrell's Blues," from William Barrell, Colonel of the regiment in 1740, and its facings. The title of "The King's Own" was conferred by George I in 1715.

(*Depot*, Newcastle-on-Tyne.)
(*Record Office*, York.)
"Wilhelmstahl," "St. Lucia, 1778," "Roliça," "Vimiera," "Corunna," "Busaco," "Ciudad Rodrigo," "Badajoz," "Salamanca," "Vittoria," "Nivelle," "Orthes," "Toulouse," "Peninsula," "Lucknow," "Afghanistan, 1878-80," "Khartoum," "Modder River," "South Africa, 1899-1902."

Motto: *Quo fata vocant* (Whither the fates call).
Uniform, Scarlet.
Facings, Gosling green.
Head-dress, Racoon-skin cap.
Plume, Scarlet, with white base, worn on left side.
Cap, Blue.
Regimental March, "British Grenadiers."
A third Colour is carried on ceremonial occasions by the drummers to commemorate the capture of a colour at Wilhelmstahl.

THE NORTHUMBERLAND FUSILIERS

Raised in 1674 the regiment was in 1764 nicknamed the "Shiners" from its smart and clean appearance; and whilst in the Peninsula was called the "Old and Bold," "The Fighting Fifth," and also "Lord Wellington's Bodyguard." It formed part of a small force which beat off an overwhelming body of the enemy at El Boden in 1811, a performance which Wellington notified to the Army as "a memorable example of what can be done by steadiness, discipline, and confidence." A custom, which has long prevailed in this regiment, is for all ranks to wear roses in their caps on St. George's Day. Among the "men" who have served in the ranks was Phœbe Hassell, the famous female soldier, afterwards pensioned by George IV, and to whose memory there is a stone in the churchyard at Hove, Brighton.

(*Depot*, Warwick.)
(*Record Office*, Warwick.)
"Namur, 1695," "Martinique, 1794," "Roliça," "Vimiera," "Corunna," "Vittoria," "Pyrenees," "Nivelle," "Orthes," "Peninsula," "Niagara," "South Africa, 1846-7, 1851-2-3," "Atbara," "Khartoum," "South Africa, 1899-1902."
Uniform, Scarlet.
Facings, Blue.
Head-dress, Helmet.
Cap, Blue with scarlet band.
Regimental March, "Warwickshire Lads."
The regiment is one of the very few bearing a battle honour won in Canada, that of "Niagara."

THE ROYAL WARWICKSHIRE REGIMENT

The regiment has a very ancient history, having existed for some time before being brought on the British establishment in 1688. It fought at Namur in 1695, and in 1707 was one of the regiments cut up at the fierce battle of Almanza. It won much distinction at the battle of Saragossa, and Colonel Harrison, who then commanded, was, as a mark of honour to the regiment, sent home with thirty standards, taken that day, to lay before the Sovereign. Tradition has it that one was the standard belonging to a Moorish Regiment in the Spanish pay, bearing an Antelope, and that that badge was forthwith conferred on the regiment. It won great fame during the Peninsular War. In the action at Echalar, 2nd August, 1813, its conduct was described by Wellington as "the most gallant and the finest thing he had ever witnessed." The title "Royal" was conferred in 1832.

It was nicknamed "Guise's Geese," also "The Warwickshire Lads," and "The Saucy Sixth."

(*Depot*, Hounslow.)

(*Record Office*, Hounslow.)

"Namur, 1695," "Martinique, 1809," "Talavera," "Busaco," "Albuhera," "Badajoz," "Salamanca," "Vittoria," "Pyrenees," "Orthes," "Toulouse," "Peninsula," "Alma," "Inkerman," "Sevastopol," "Kandahar, 1880," "Afghanistan, 1879-80," "Relief of Ladysmith," "South Africa, 1899-1902."

Uniform, Scarlet.

Facings, Blue.

Head-dress, Racoon-skin cap, with white plume on right side.

Cap, Blue, with scarlet band.

Regimental March, "British Grenadiers."

Until after the Crimean War there were no 2nd Lieutenants or Ensigns in this regiment. The regiment has the privilege of marching through the City of London with fixed bayonets, drums beating, and colours flying.

THE ROYAL FUSILIERS (City of London Regiment)

Raised in 1685. In the Peninsular War it took a glorious part, and no troops hazarded their lives more freely for their country's cause, than the Royal Fusiliers. At Talavera they met the storm of war with unshaken firmness, and captured seven of the enemy's guns, but the undying lustre of the glory they won at Albuhera, almost overshadows their other gallant exploits at this time. They had marched from Badajos at 2 a.m. the same day, and the night march of 20 miles, followed by the supreme effort which regained the lost heights of Albuhera, must rank as an unsurpassed feat of arms. During the Crimean War the conduct of the Royal Fusiliers won further glory.

It was once known as "The Hanoverian White Horse," and also as the "Elegant Extracts" from the fact that the officers were selected from other corps.

**The Royal Fusiliers marching through the City of London.
Presentation of Colours.**

(*Depot*, Seaforth.)

(*Record Office*, Preston.)

The Sphinx, superscribed "Egypt."

"Blenheim," "Ramillies," "Oudenarde," "Malplaquet," "Dettingen," "Martinique, 1809," "Niagara," "Delhi, 1857," "Lucknow," "Peiwar Kotal," "Afghanistan, 1878-80," "Burma, 1885-87," "Defence of Ladysmith," "South Africa, 1899-1902."

Motto: *Nec aspera terrent* (Nor do difficulties deter).

Uniform, Scarlet.

Facings, Blue.

Head-dress, Helmet.

Cap, Blue with red band.

Regimental March, "Here's to the maiden of bashful fifteen."

Allied Regiment, 8th Australian Infantry Regiment.

THE KING'S (LIVERPOOL REGIMENT)

Raised in 1685. It gained considerable reputation during Marlborough's campaign when it was known as the "Queen's," but on George I's accession it became "The King's," a proud title which it still keeps and by which it is known. It fought at Dettingen in 1743, memorable as being the last battle in which a British King led his army in person. It was stationed at Jullundur on the outbreak of the Indian Mutiny. A detachment of the regiment performed an important service by securing the fort and magazine at Phillour. They marched from Jullundur to Delhi, in fourteen days, and with bayonet and rifle helped to clear the city of the mutineers. They took part in the relief of Agra, where they defeated 8,000 mutineers and captured all their guns. They then proceeded to the relief of Lucknow and took part in other operations.

Nickname: "The Leather Hats."

(*Depot*, Norwich.)

(*Record Office*, Warley.)

"Havannah," "Martinique, 1794," "Roliça," "Vimiera," "Corunna," "Busaco," "Salamanca," "Vittoria," "St. Sebastian," "Nive," "Peninsula," "Cabool, 1842," "Moodkee," "Ferozeshah," "Sobraon," "Sevastopol," "Kabul, 1879," "Afghanistan,

1879-80," "Paardeberg," "South Africa, 1900-02."
Uniform, Scarlet.
Facings, Yellow.
Head-dress, Helmet.
Cap, Blue.
Regimental March, "Rule Britannia."
Allied Regiment: 9th Australian Infantry Regiment.

THE NORFOLK REGIMENT

Formed in 1695. The "Figure of Britannia" was awarded as a regimental badge to commemorate its heroic struggle against overwhelming numbers at the battle of Almanza. It won much glory during the Peninsular War. At Roleia it bore the brunt of the enemy's attack, and at Corunna, where the gallant Sir John Moore met a soldier's death, to the regiment fell the melancholy honour of placing him in a soldier's grave. In the Afghan War of 1842, and in the Sikh War of 1845 its bravery was conspicuous. At Ferozeshah the Sikhs had 100 guns, which they served with great effect, repulsing the first attack; but the Ninth restored the day, bayoneting the Sikhs at their guns, and driving the enemy before them.

Nicknames: "The Holy Boys," a name given them by the Spanish during the Peninsular War, from the fact that they wore the figure of Britannia on their cross-belts, which the Spaniards took to represent the Virgin Mary; also "The Fighting Ninth," and "The Norfolk Howards."

(*Depot*, Lincoln.)
(*Record Office*, Lichfield.)
The Sphinx, superscribed "Egypt."
"Blenheim," "Ramillies," "Oudenarde," "Malplaquet," "Peninsula," "Sobraon," "Mooltan," "Goojerat," "Punjaub," "Lucknow," "Atbara," "Khartoum," "Paardeberg," "South Africa, 1900-02."
Uniform, Scarlet.
Facings, White.
Head-dress, Helmet.
Cap, Blue.
Regimental March, "The Lincolnshire Poacher."
When first raised was the only blue coated infantry regiment.
Allied Regiment: 19th "Lincoln" Regiment of Canada.

THE LINCOLNSHIRE REGIMENT

Formed from an Independent Company in 1685. It fought with distinction during Marlborough's campaign. Of its conduct in the Sikh War the Brigadier said, "The glorious conduct of the regiment at Sobraon is beyond any praise I could give—it was the corner stone of the victory."

During the Indian Mutiny it assisted to save Benares and Dinapore from the Sepoys and to bring the final rescue to the heroic defenders of Lucknow. The regiment took part in the famous march on Khartoum and in the battle of Atbara and Omdurman which broke the power of the Mahdi and placed Soudan under British control. It was also in the South African War, and again added to its fine reputation.

It was (with the 62nd) nicknamed "The Springers," during the American War, from their readiness for action. "The Poachers" in allusion to the famous old ballad, which is played as the Regimental March.

(*Depot*, Exeter.)
(*Record Office*, Exeter.)
"Dettingen," "Salamanca," "Pyrenees," "Nivelle," "Nive," "Orthes," "Toulouse," "Peninsula," "Afghanistan, 1879-80," "Tirah," "Defence of Ladysmith," "Relief of Ladysmith," "South Africa, 1899-1902."
Motto: *Semper Fidelis* (Ever faithful).
Uniform, Scarlet.
Facings, Lincoln Green.
Head-dress, Helmet.
Cap, Blue.
Regimental March, "We've lived and loved together."

The Regimental March owes its origin to a circumstance prior to the Battle of Salamanca. The 11th found itself marching in close proximity to a French regiment. As no order to attack was given, the officers on either side saluted by lowering their swords, and at parting the British bandsmen struck up, out of compliment to their adversaries, the tune in question.

THE DEVONSHIRE REGIMENT

Formed in 1685. It displayed splendid bravery but was cut to pieces at Almanza in 1707. During the Peninsular War it gained great distinction. At Salamanca, the fierce character of the struggle may be gathered from the fact that only four officers and sixty-seven men of the regiment could be mustered at the close of the action, to hear, however, words of praise seldom addressed to an individual regiment. At Toulouse for the second time during the war it shared in the supreme effort which turned the tide of victory. No record of the Devons would be complete which omitted the supreme gallantry of the regiment in the desperate fighting at Wagon Hill during the South African War.

Nickname: "The Bloody Eleventh," from the number of casualties at the battle of Salamanca.

Colonel Ridge leading the stormers at Badajoz.
Private, 1750. Officer, 1780. Sergeant, 1807. Private, 1835.
Types of old Infantry Uniforms.

(*Depot*, Bury St. Edmunds.)
(*Record Office*, Warley.)
The Castle and Key, superscribed "Gibraltar, 1779-83."
"Dettingen," "Minden," "Seringapatam," "India," "South Africa, 1851-2-3," "New Zealand," "Afghanistan, 1878-80," "South Africa, 1899-1902."
Uniform, Scarlet.
Facings, Yellow.
Head-dress, Helmet.
Cap, Blue.
Regimental March, "Speed the plough."
Allied Regiment, 3rd (Auckland) Regiment ("Countess of Ranfurly's Own"), New Zealand.

THE SUFFOLK REGIMENT

Formed in 1685. At Dettingen, under King George II, it took part in the final charge which assured the victory—the last occasion on which a British King personally commanded his troops in action. It was one of the six British Infantry regiments which at Minden shattered the French cavalry, and finally drove out of the field every body of troops opposed to them. The Duke of Brunswick who commanded the forces said: "It was here the British Infantry gained immortal glory." Its services in the defence of Gibraltar are commemorated by the Castle and Key and Motto. At the storming of Seringapatam it captured eight stands of colours. For this splendid behaviour during their two years' defence of Gibraltar was given the crest and motto they now wear.

Nickname: The "Old Dozen." The men wear roses in their caps on August 1st in commemoration of the Battle of Minden, 1759.

(*Depot*, Taunton.)
(*Record Office*, Exeter.)
The Sphinx, superscribed "Egypt."A Mural Crown, superscribed "Jellalabad."
"Gibraltar, 1704-5," "Dettingen," "Martinique, 1809," "Ava," "Ghuznee, 1839," "Affghanistan, 1839," "Cabool, 1842," "Sevastopol," "South Africa, 1878-9," "Burmah, 1885-87," "Relief of Ladysmith," "South Africa, 1899-1902."
Uniform, Scarlet.
Facings, Blue.
Head-dress, Helmet.
Cap, Dark green.
Regimental March, "Prince Albert's March."
Allied Regiment, 13th "Royal Regiment" of Canada.
The Sergeants wear the sash on the left shoulder in memory of the Battle of Culloden, where all the officers fell and the remnant of the regiment was brought out of action by the surviving sergeants. This is the only regiment in the service not designated "Royal" wearing Royal Blue facings.

PRINCE ALBERT'S (Somerset Light Infantry)

Raised in 1685. While fighting in Spain, 1706-13, the regiment fought as dragoons. It earned a brilliant record in Afghanistan, 1839-42. After storming Ghuznee it was ordered to Jellalabad which detached post it gallantly held. The massacre of the Cabul force inspired the Afghans to fiercer efforts against Jellalabad; but in spite of news of disaster, the enemy, and even nature itself,—for over 100 shocks of earthquake shook the ruined walls—the brave Somersets defied them all. At length they sallied out and decisively defeated the Afghans. This "Illustrious Garrison," as it was termed by the Government of India, was received on its return by special honours in all cantonments through which it passed. For its services it received its present title, and a mural crown superscribed "Jellalabad."

Nicknamed "The Bleeders."

(*Depot*, York.)
(*Record Office*, York.)
The Royal Tiger, superscribed "India."
"Namur, 1695," "Tournay," "Corunna," "Java," "Waterloo," "Bhurtpore," "Sevastopol," "New Zealand," "Afghanistan, 1879-80," "Relief of Ladysmith," "South Africa, 1899-1902."
Motto: *Nec aspera terrent* (Nor do difficulties deter).

Uniform, Scarlet.
Facings, Buff.
Head-dress, Helmet.
Cap, Blue.
Regimental March, "Ça ira."
Allied Regiment, 16th (Waikato) Regiment of New Zealand.

THE PRINCE OF WALES'S OWN (West Yorkshire Regiment)

Raised in 1685. It shared in the defence of Gibraltar in 1727, and added very considerably to its laurels in the wars of 1793-4. In an attack on the French camp at Famars, 23rd May, 1793, it not only gained a victory, but also its regimental march. Among the pieces of music which fanned the fiery zeal of the French was "Ça ira," to the strains of which they hurled themselves with impetuosity on the British troops. The colonel however, with a magnificent inspiration called out to his men "Come along, my lads, we'll break them to their own d——d tune," and bade his drummers strike up "Ça ira." The effect was irresistible, and the French found themselves flying from the sound of their own martial air. The regiment fought with characteristic bravery at Corunna, in Java, at Waterloo, in India, in the Crimea, New Zealand, and South Africa, reaping the highest commendation for gallantry and devotion everywhere.

Nicknames: "The Old and Bold" and "Calvert's Entire."

(*Depot*, Beverley.)
(*Record Office*, York.)
"Blenheim," "Ramillies," "Oudenarde," "Malplaquet," "Louisburg," "Quebec, 1759," "Martinique, 1762," "Havannah," "St. Lucia, 1778," "Martinique 1794, 1809," "Guadaloupe, 1810," "Afghanistan, 1879-80," "South Africa, 1900-02."
Uniform, Scarlet.
Facings, White.
Head-dress, Helmet.
Cap, Blue.
Regimental March, "Yorkshire Lass."
The officers wear a black line in the top and bottom of the lace, as a memento of General Wolfe's death.

EAST YORKSHIRE REGIMENT

Raised in 1685. The regiment went to Holland with Marlborough, and bore a distinguished part in all his campaigns. It was one of the five regiments which commenced the battle of Blenheim by an attack on the entrenched village of that name, moving up steadily under a withering fire without returning a shot, until their leader, General Rowe, struck his sword into the palisades. It fought at Ramillies, at Oudenarde, and at Malplaquet, and bore an active part at Tournay. It went to Quebec with Wolfe, who specially commended the steadiness of the regiment. It fought in the great battle on the heights of Abraham, and after Wolfe's fall served in the conquest of Canada. Has a splendid record of bravery in many other battles.

Nicknames: "The Snappers," from an incident in the American War, where, the ammunition having given out, they continued to snap their firelocks with undaunted determination. The enemy retired, misled by their aspect and bravery; also called the "Poona Guards."

(*Depot*, Bedford.)
(*Record Office*, Warley.)
"Namur, 1695," "Blenheim," "Ramillies," "Oudenarde," "Malplaquet," "Surinam," "Chitral," "South Africa, 1900-02."
Uniform, Scarlet.
Facings, White.
Head-dress, Helmet.
Cap, Blue.
Regimental March, "Mountain Rose."

BEDFORDSHIRE REGIMENT

Raised in 1688. It served all through Marlborough's campaigns, and its gallant conduct in no less than thirty-four successful battles and sieges firmly established its reputation. It was at the siege of Lille, where one of the sergeants, Littler, performed gallant service by swimming the river with a hatchet, and, in the face of the enemy single handed cut the fastenings of a drawbridge. It took part in the battle of Dettingen, where the French generously commended their bravery, and declared they saw them advancing, not like men, but devils, in the face of whole batteries, which fired directly into them, sweeping down all ranks without being able to break them. As part of the Chitral Relief Expedition it took part in the storming of the Malakand Pass. This expedition was an example of sturdy perseverance in the face of obstacles, which it is not possible for those who have not served on the Northern Frontier of India to realise.

Nicknames: "The Old Bucks"; also known as "The Peacemakers," from the ferocity with which it was wont to attack the enemy, who were generally glad to quickly make peace.

(*Depot*, Leicester.)
(*Record Office*, Lichfield.)
The Royal Tiger, superscribed "Hindoostan."
"Namur, 1695," "Louisburg," "Martinique, 1762," "Havannah," "Ghuznee, 1839," "Khelat," "Affghanistan, 1839," "Sevastopol," "Ali Masjid," "Afghanistan, 1878-79," "Defence of Ladysmith," "South Africa, 1899-1902."
Uniform, Scarlet.
Facings, White.
Head-dress, Helmet.
Cap, Blue.
Regimental March, "Romaika."
The officers wear a black line in their lace to commemorate the death of General Wolfe at Quebec, and the band always plays "Wolfe's Lament," immediately before the National Anthem.

LEICESTERSHIRE REGIMENT

Raised in 1688. It took part in the earlier portion of Marlborough's campaigns and then proceeded to Spain, where it fought at the battle of Almanza with desperate courage against overwhelming numbers. It also took part in the conquest of Canada. In 1804 it proceeded to India, where, during a period of 18 years, it took a distinguished part in building up our mighty Indian Empire. Its services were specially acknowledged by the grant of the badge of the "Royal Tiger" with the word "Hindoostan," as a lasting testimony of the exemplary conduct of all ranks during its service in India from 1804 to 1823. In 1838 it was with the army which forced its way through Scinde capturing Hyderabad and Kurrachee.

Nicknames: "Lily Whites," from their facings; also "Bengal Tigers," from its badge, a Royal Tiger.

(*Depot*, Clonmel.)
(*Record Office*, Cork.)
The Sphinx, superscribed "Egypt." The Dragon, superscribed "China."
"Namur, 1695," "Blenheim," "Ramillies," "Oudenarde," "Malplaquet," "Pegu," "Sevastopol," "New Zealand," "Afghanistan, 1879-80," "Tel-el-Kebir," "Egypt, 1882," "Nile, 1884-85," "South Africa, 1900-02."
Motto: *Virtutis Namurcensis Præmium* (The Reward of Valour at Namur).

Uniform, Scarlet.
Facings, Blue.
Head-dress, Helmet.
Cap, Blue with scarlet band.
Regimental March, "Garry Owen."
Allied Regiment, 7th (Wellington West Coast) Regiment of New Zealand.

THE ROYAL IRISH REGIMENT

Raised in 1683. After serving afloat as Marines it went to Flanders, where its splendid valour at the assault on the Castle of Namur on 20th August, 1695, won for it the admiration of the whole of the Allied army. This gallant feat, performed under the eyes of the King, won for the regiment the distinguished title of the Royal Regiment of Foot of Ireland, and the King conferred upon it the right of displaying the badge of the harp and crown, and that of the lion of Nassau, with the motto "Virtutis Namurcensis Præmium." Was one of the Irish Regiments which fought so gallantly in South Africa and to whose bravery the Irish Guards were raised in commemoration. "The Royal Irish" is the only one now in existence out of nineteen regiments raised in Ireland from independent companies of musketeers and pikemen.

Nicknames: "The Namurs," and "Paddy's Blackguards."

(*Depot*, Richmond.)
(*Record Office*, York.)
"Malplaquet," "Alma," "Inkerman," "Sevastopol," "Tirah," "Relief of Kimberley," "Paardeberg," "South Africa, 1899-1902."
Uniform, Scarlet.
Facings, Grass green.
Head-dress, Helmet.
Cap, Blue.
Regimental March, "Bonnie English Rose."

ALEXANDRA, PRINCESS OF WALES'S OWN
(Yorkshire Regiment)

Raised in 1688. Its first services were in Flanders, where it fought at the siege and capture of Namur. It took part in the most sanguinary of Marlborough's victories, the battle of Malplaquet, besides engaging in several of the sieges which constituted the latter part of the campaign. The massacre in Ceylon of a detachment of the regiment, consisting of 178 officers and men, forms one of the most tragic episodes in military history. The remainder of the regiment was speedily in the field to avenge those slaughtered, and an ample retribution was exacted from the treacherous Candyans. During the Crimean war it nobly upheld its reputation, and the regiment fought with splendid bravery in the Tirah campaign, and in South Africa, being present at the relief of Kimberley, and the battle of Paardeberg. It added to its great name in the great war on the Continent.

Nickname: "The Green Howards," from its facings, and the name of its first Colonel.

Drums and Silver-mounted Drum-Major's Staff taken by the 2nd Battalion of the 34th Regiment (Border Regiment) from the 34th Regiment of French Infantry of the Line, during the Peninsular War, at the Battle of Arroyo-dos-Molinos, 28th October, 1811.

The Lancashire Fusiliers.—Returning from a Review.

(*Depot*, Bury.)

(*Record Office*, Preston.)

The Sphinx, superscribed "Egypt."

"Dettingen," "Minden," "Egmont-op-Zee," "Maida," "Vimiera," "Corunna," "Vittoria," "Pyrenees," "Orthes," "Toulouse," "Peninsula," "Alma," "Inkerman," "Sevastopol," "Lucknow," "Khartoum," "Relief of Ladysmith," "South Africa, 1899-1902."

Motto: *Omnia Audax* (Daring Everything).

Uniform, Scarlet.

Facings, White.

Head-dress, Racoon-skin cap with primrose plume on left side.

Cap, Blue.

Regimental March, "British Grenadiers."

THE LANCASHIRE FUSILIERS

Raised in 1688. It won lasting fame on the historic field of Minden. So heavy were its losses on that day that Prince Ferdinand directed the regiment to be excused from further duty. This they declined to accept, and a General Order records that "Kingsley's Regiment, at its own request, will resume its portion of duty in the line." In addition to the battle honour a laurel wreath was ordered to be worn on the colours and appointments. These glorious memories are recalled by the regimental custom of wearing "Minden Roses" in the caps on each 1st August. Its bravery throughout the Peninsular War was conspicuous, and the Duke of Wellington, when presenting it with Colours in 1838, said: "I declare that of the many distinguished regiments of the

British Army, which I have had the honour to command, this, the best and most distinguished, is entitled to all the eulogiums I may have bestowed upon it."

Nicknames: The "Two Tens" from its number, also "The Minden Boys," and "Kingsley's Stand."

(*Depot*, Ayr.)
(*Record Office*, Hamilton.)
"Blenheim," "Ramillies," "Oudenarde," "Malplaquet," "Dettingen," "Martinique, 1794," "Bladensburg," "Alma," "Inkerman," "Sevastopol," "South Africa, 1879," "Burma, 1885-87," "Tirah," "Relief of Ladysmith," "South Africa, 1899-1902."
Motto: *Nemo me impune lacessit* (No one provokes me with impunity).
Uniform, Scarlet.
Facings, Blue.
Trews, of Sutherland tartan.
Head-dress, Sealskin cap with white plume on right side.
Cap, Glengarry, with scarlet, white and green diced border.
Regimental March, "British Grenadiers."

THE ROYAL SCOTS FUSILIERS

Raised in 1678. It was one of the brave battalions which steadily marched to the attack on the village of Blenheim until the palisades were reached, without firing a shot in reply to the tempest of shot which greeted them. At Ramillies, at Oudenarde, on the red field of Malplaquet, the most fiercely fought of Marlborough's victories, and in numerous minor engagements, its conduct was ever conspicuous. Under the brave "Sheriff" Agnew,—the Sir Andrew Agnew whose name is familiar to readers of Scott,—it fought at Dettingen. The regiment delivered a volley, and charged the cavalry with the bayonet, nearly annihilating a French corps. King George II. witnessed the movement and its result, and praised all ranks for their great gallantry. The regiment has fought in all parts of the world since, and with equal distinction.

Nicknamed: "Earl of Mar's Grey Breeks," from the colour of the men's breeches at the time the regiment was raised (1678).

(*Depot*, Chester.)
(*Record Office*, Shrewsbury.)
"Louisburg," "Martinique, 1762," "Havannah," "Meeanee," "Hyderabad," "Scinde," "South Africa, 1900-02."
Uniform, Scarlet.

Facings, Buff.
Head-dress, Helmet.
Cap, Blue.
Regimental March, "Wha wadna' fecht for Charlie."

THE CHESHIRE REGIMENT

Raised in 1689, and was present at the battle of Dettingen, where King George II commanded in person. The King was at one time hotly pressed by the French cavalry, when a detachment formed round him under an oak tree and drove the enemy away. The King plucked a leaf off the tree and, handing it to the commander, desired the regiment to wear it in memory of their gallant conduct. The oakleaf is now worn in the head-dress, and on the colours on September 12th, and on ceremonial parades. In 1795 it recruited its ranks with poorhouse boys between the ages of twelve and sixteen. Amongst the boys who joined was John Shipp, an orphan, who performed the unique feat of *twice* winning a commission from the ranks before he was thirty years old, for conspicuous bravery in the field. In 1843 it formed part of the force under Sir Charles Napier which destroyed the Indian desert stronghold of Emaun Ghur—an enterprise characterised as one of the most curious and dangerous military feats ever known.

Nicknames: The "Two Twos"; also in 1795 the "Red Knights," from being served out with all red clothing; also known as the "Lightning Conductors."

(*Depot*, Wrexham.)
(*Record Office*, Shrewsbury.)
The Sphinx, superscribed "Egypt."
"Namur, 1695," "Blenheim," "Ramillies," "Oudenarde," "Malplaquet," "Dettingen," "Minden," "Corunna," "Martinique, 1809," "Albuhera," "Badajoz," "Salamanca," "Vittoria," "Pyrenees," "Nivelle," "Orthes," "Toulouse," "Peninsula," "Waterloo," "Alma," "Inkerman," "Sevastopol," "Lucknow," "Ashantee, 1873-4," "Burma, 1885-87," "Relief of Ladysmith," "South Africa, 1899-1902," "Pekin, 1900."
Motto: *Nec aspera terrent* (Difficulties do not dismay us).
Uniform, Scarlet.
Facings, Blue.
Head-dress, Racoon-skin cap with white plume on right side.
Cap, Blue with scarlet band.
Regimental March, "British Grenadiers."
All ranks wear "The Flash," a bow of broad black silk ribbon with long ends attached to the back of the tunic collar.

THE ROYAL WELSH FUSILIERS

Raised in 1689. In the Crimean War, at Alma it captured a Russian gun, which is now at the Depot, Wrexham. It was during this action that Sergeant Luke O'Connor gained his Victoria Cross and a commission, and lived to attain the rank of General. The regiment has fought in all parts of the world and has a splendid roll of battle honours.

Nicknamed "The Nanny Goats" and "The Royal Goats," from its custom of having a goat led at the head of the drums. Regimental custom prescribes that on St. David's night, the 1st of March, every officer or guest who has never eaten a leek before, shall eat one, standing in his chair with one foot on the table, while a drummer beats a roll behind him.

L'entente cordiale.
1694. 1747. 1808. *Present Day.*
Types of Uniforms worn by The Worcestershire Regiment.

(*Depot*, Brecon.)

(*Record Office*, Shrewsbury.)

The Sphinx, superscribed "Egypt."

"Blenheim," "Ramillies," "Oudenarde," "Malplaquet," "Cape of Good Hope, 1806," "Talavera," "Busaco," "Fuentes d'Onor," "Salamanca," "Vittoria," "Pyrenees," "Nivelle," "Orthes," "Peninsula," "Chillianwallah," "Goojerat," "Punjaub," "South Africa, 1877-8-9," "Burma, 1885-87," "South Africa, 1900-02."

Uniform, Scarlet.

Facings, Grass green.

Head-dress, Helmet.

Cap, Blue.

Regimental March, "Men of Harlech."

A silver wreath is borne on the staff of the King's Colour of both battalions to commemorate the devoted gallantry of Lieutenants Melville and Coghill in saving that colour from the hands of the Zulus, after the Battle of Isandlwana, and as a tribute of appreciation of the gallant defence of Rorke's Drift, 1879.

THE SOUTH WALES BORDERERS

Raised in 1689, the regiment has one of the most remarkable histories in the British Army, having twice being almost annihilated, at Chillianwallah, 1849, where 23 officers and 527 men were killed and wounded, the regiment being brought out of action by the quartermaster; and in 1879 at Isandlwana, where hardly a man escaped death. The gallant defence of Rorke's Drift by one company roused the wonder and admiration of the whole civilised world. The losses of the regiment in killed alone reached the appalling total of 21 officers and 590 men. It had the proud distinction of having won more Victoria Crosses than any other corps in the British Army.

Nicknamed "Howard's Greens," from its facings and its Colonel's name from 1717 to 1737.

(*Depot*, Berwick-on-Tweed.)
(*Record Office*, Hamilton.)
The Sphinx, superscribed "Egypt."
"Namur, 1695," "Minden," "Egmont-op-Zee," "Martinique, 1809," "Afghanistan, 1878-80," "Chitral," "Tirah," "Paardeberg," "South Africa, 1900-02."
Mottoes: *Nisi Dominus frustra* (Without the Lord all your efforts are vain); *In Veritate Religionis confido* (I trust in the truth of religion); *Nec aspera terrent* (Nor do difficulties deter).
Uniform, Scarlet doublet, with trews of Leslie tartan, the pipers being kilted and wearing the Royal Stewart tartan.
Head-dress, Blue Kilmarnock Bonnet, with black plume.
Cap, Glengarry, with scarlet, white and green diced border.
Regimental March, "Blue bonnets over the border."

THE KING'S OWN SCOTTISH BORDERERS

Raised in 1689, in the space of four hours, by the Earl of Leven, in Edinburgh. At the siege of Namur, one of the strongest fortresses in Europe, it lost 20 officers and 500 men by the explosion of one of the enemy's mines. The Borderers, however, quickly recovered and routed the enemy at the point of the bayonet. The regiment was also one of the gallant six to participate in the glorious victory at Minden. Acting as Marines it participated in Lord Howe's glorious victory of 1st June, 1794. It has also fought with great credit in other parts of the world.

They were sometimes called "The Botherers," and commonly "K.O.S.B's." Also nicknamed the "Kokky-Olly Birds." This regiment has the exclusive privilege of beating up for recruits in the streets of Edinburgh at any time without asking the leave of the Lord Provost.

(*Depot*, Hamilton.)
(*Record Office*, Hamilton.)

The Sphinx, superscribed "Egypt." The Dragon, superscribed "China."
"Blenheim," "Ramillies," "Oudenarde," "Malplaquet," "Mandora," "Corunna," "Martinique, 1809," "Guadaloupe, 1810," "South Africa, 1846-7," "Sevastopol," "Lucknow," "Abyssinia," "South Africa, 1877-8-9," "Relief of Ladysmith," "South Africa, 1899-1902."

Uniform, Dark green doublet with green facings and trews of Douglas tartan.
Head-dress, Green chaco with black plume.
Cap, Green glengarry.
Regimental March, "Within a mile of Edinboro' town."

THE CAMERONIANS (SCOTTISH RIFLES)

The Cameronians date from the revolution of 1688, twenty companies of sixty men being raised within the space of 24 hours. Proceeding to Flanders it fought bravely and with much distinction during Marlborough's campaigns. It was engaged in the capture of Martinique and Guadaloupe, where among other trophies of victory it took an "Eagle," the regimental standard of the French. It bore a distinguished part in the Crimean War. It also took part in the hottest fighting in the Mutiny and in the march through Abyssinia, and fought with great gallantry in the Zulu and South African campaigns. Two of our most distinguished Field-Marshals—Lord Wolseley, V.C., and Sir Evelyn Wood, V.C., served in this regiment.

Nicknames: 1st Battalion "The Cameronians," and the 2nd Battalion "Perthshire Grey Breeks," from the colour of the men's breeches.

(*Depot*, Omagh.)
(*Record Office*, Dublin.)
The Sphinx, superscribed "Egypt."
"Martinique, 1762," "Havannah," "St. Lucia, 1778, 1796," "Maida," "Badajoz," "Salamanca," "Vittoria," "Pyrenees," "Nivelle," "Orthes," "Toulouse," "Peninsula," "Waterloo," "South Africa, 1835, 1846-7," "Central India," "Relief of Ladysmith," "South Africa, 1899-1902."

Motto: *Nec aspera terrent* (Nor do difficulties deter).
Uniform, Scarlet.
Facings, Blue.
Head-dress, Racoon-skin cap with grey plume on left side.
Cap, Blue, with scarlet band.
Regimental March, "British Grenadiers."
The regiment was the first to introduce the Irish war pipe into the Army.

THE ROYAL INNISKILLING FUSILIERS

Formed in 1689. Proceeding to the West Indies it greatly distinguished itself at the storming and capture of the citadel of St. Lucia. In recognition of "the steady and intrepid bearing of the officers and men of the regiment," Sir Ralph Abercromby directed that the garrison on marching out should lay down their arms to the Inniskillings. During the Peninsular War, at Castella, a French officer advancing in front of the line, challenged anyone in the regiment to single combat. His wish was immediately complied with by Captain Waldron, who after a few passes, laid the Frenchman dead. The Inniskillings then dashed forward with the bayonet, and the enemy broke and fled before their irresistible onslaught. The regiment has reaped honour and glory in all parts of the world.

The 2nd Battalion were nicknamed "The Lumps."

(*Depot*, Bristol.)
(*Record Office*, Warwick.)
The Sphinx, superscribed "Egypt."
"Ramillies," "Louisburg," "Guadaloupe, 1759," "Quebec, 1759," "Martinique, 1762," "Havannah," "St. Lucia, 1778," "Maida," "Corunna," "Talavera," "Busaco," "Barrosa," "Albuhera," "Salamanca," "Vittoria," "Pyrenees," "Nivelle," "Nive," "Orthes," "Toulouse," "Peninsula," "Waterloo," "Chillianwallah," "Goojerat," "Punjaub," "Alma," "Inkerman," "Sevastopol," "Delhi, 1857," "Defence of Ladysmith," "Relief of Kimberley," "Paardeberg," "South Africa, 1899-1902."

Uniform, Scarlet.
Facings, White.
Head-dress, Helmet.
Cap, Blue.
Regimental March, "Kynegad Slashers."

GLOUCESTERSHIRE REGIMENT

Raised in 1694, and has fought with the highest credit in all parts of the Empire, during which it has won several peculiar and highly cherished distinctions. Of its conduct at Chillianwallah the Duke of Wellington said, "the 61st were mainly instrumental in gaining the victory."

The 28th Regiment was nicknamed "The Old Braggs" in 1750, from its Colonel's name, General Philip Braggs. Also the "Slashers," from their gallantry at the battle of the White Plains, and passage of the Brunx river in 1777. A badge is worn on the back of the head-dress by both battalions of this regiment, given for the bravery of the 28th at Alexandria in 1801. They were attacked by French cavalry while in line, and there being no time to form square, the Colonel ordered the rear rank to "Right about face," and they succeeded in beating off the enemy, 7,000 in number.

Nickname: 1st Battalion "The Back Numbers."

(*Depot*, Worcester.)
(*Record Office*, Warwick.)
A Naval Crown, superscribed "1st June, 1794."
"Ramillies," "Mysore," "Hindoostan," "Roliça," "Vimiera," "Corunna," "Talavera," "Albuhera," "Salamanca," "Pyrenees," "Nivelle," "Nive," "Orthes," "Toulouse," "Peninsula," "Ferozeshah," "Sobraon," "Chillianwallah," "Goojerat," "Punjaub," "South Africa, 1900-02."
Motto: *Firm*.
Uniform, Scarlet.
Facings, White.
Head-dress, Helmet.
Cap, Blue.
Regimental March, "The Windsor."

WORCESTERSHIRE REGIMENT

The regiment was raised in 1694 and won in action one of the proudest mottoes ever bestowed on a regiment, that of "Firm." The 29th was the last of the regiments in the Peninsula to retain the queue, in which the men fought at Vimiera, the officers wearing the old fashioned and picturesque cocked hats.

Nicknames: "The Ever-sworded 29th" owing to a peculiar custom, which demands that the captain and subaltern of the day shall dine with their swords on. Up to the fifties all the officers sat down to dinner wearing their weapons, the custom having originated in 1746, when a part of the regiment, stationed at the Leeward Islands, was surprised without its arms, and treacherously murdered by the Indians. The "Vein Openers," given on account of its being the first to draw blood, in 1770, when the disturbances, which preceded the outbreak of the American War, commenced. They are also known as the "Old and Bold," "The Star of the Line," and "The Saucy Greens."

(*Depot*, Preston.)
(*Record Office*, Preston.)

The Sphinx, superscribed "Egypt."
"Gibraltar, 1704-5," "Cape of Good Hope, 1806," "Corunna," "Java," "Badajoz," "Salamanca," "Vittoria," "St. Sebastian," "Nive," "Peninsula," "Waterloo," "Bhurtpore," "Alma," "Inkerman," "Sevastopol," "Canton," "Ahmad Khel," "Afghanistan, 1878-80," "Chitral," "South Africa, 1900-02."

Motto: *Spectamur Agendo* (We are judged by our actions).
Uniform, Scarlet.
Facings, White.
Head-dress, Helmet.
Cap, Blue.
Regimental March, "Lancashire Lads."

EAST LANCASHIRE REGIMENT

Raised in 1694. When first formed it saw much eventful service as Marines, and served in the capture of Gibraltar in 1704, and in the great sea-fight off Malaga which followed. In January 1816, a battalion of the 59th was wrecked while proceeding to Ireland, and nearly the whole of the men perished. At Waterloo, after the British squares reformed line to make the final advance, the regiment left its formation plainly marked on the ground it had occupied by the square of dead and dying comrades who had fallen in the grim opposition to the enemy's cavalry and artillery. It fought with great distinction in the Crimea, China, Afghanistan and South Africa, winning the highest commendations everywhere.

Nicknamed: "The Triple Xs," also "The Three Tens." 59th Foot, "Lily Whites," from its facings.

(*Depot*, Kingston.)
(*Record Office*, Hounslow.)
"Gibraltar, 1704-5," "Dettingen," "Martinique, 1794," "Talavera," "Guadaloupe, 1810," "Albuhera," "Vittoria," "Pyrenees," "Nivelle," "Nive," "Orthes," "Peninsula," "Cabool, 1842," "Moodkee," "Ferozeshah," "Aliwal," "Sobraon," "Sevastopol," "Taku Forts," "New Zealand," "Afghanistan, 1878-79," "Suakin, 1885," "Relief of Ladysmith," "South Africa, 1899-1902."

Uniform, Scarlet.
Facings, White.
Head-dress, Helmet.
Cap, Blue.
Allied Regiment, 4th (Otago) Regiment of New Zealand.

Regimental March, "A Southerly Wind and a Cloudy Sky."

The officers wear a black line in their lace to commemorate the death of General Wolfe at Quebec.

THE EAST SURREY REGIMENT

Raised in 1702 as a corps of Marines and for many years did splendid service ashore and afloat all over the world. The burning of the "Kent," East Indiaman, with a wing of the 31st Regiment on board, in the Bay of Biscay, on 1st May, 1824, forms one of the most thrilling episodes of heroism at sea British regimental history affords. During a storm the vessel caught fire and was totally destroyed. The discipline of the men under these terrible circumstances was beyond all praise, and in a great measure owing to this fact over 550 people out of 637 were saved. In the Sikh War they captured four standards.

Nicknames: The 1st Battalion (31st Foot) was known as "The Young Buffs," to distinguish it from the 3rd (Old Buffs). The 2nd Battalion (70th Foot) was nicknamed the "Glasgow Greys."

(*Depot*, Bodmin.)
(*Record Office*, Exeter.)
"Gibraltar, 1704-05," "Dettingen," "St. Lucia, 1778," "Dominica," "Roliça," "Vimiera," "Corunna," "Salamanca," "Pyrenees," "Nivelle," "Nive," "Orthes," "Peninsula," "Waterloo," "Mooltan," "Goojerat," "Punjaub," "Sevastopol," "Lucknow," "Tel-el-Kebir," "Egypt, 1882," "Nile, 1884-85," "Paardeberg," "South Africa, 1899-1902."
Uniform, Scarlet.
Facings, White.
Head-dress, Helmet.
Cap, Green with green band.
Regimental March, "One and All."

THE DUKE OF CORNWALL'S LIGHT INFANTRY

Raised in 1702. In its early history it saw much varied service as Marines. The 2nd Battalion (46th Foot) in 1777 was called the "Red Feathers," from the following circumstances. The light company took part in an attack against General Wayne's Brigade, near Brandywine Creek, in which the Americans were surprised and utterly defeated. The Americans vowed vengeance and swore that they would give no quarter; the soldiers of the light company stained their feathers red as a distinguishing mark, so that the enemy could easily see whom to attack. This badge is still preserved in the brass feather and red cloth of the helmet and cap badge. They are also called "The Lacedemonians." The heroic defence of the Lucknow Residency, and the tragic fate of the detachment under Captain Moore, at Cawnpore, are treasured memories. The 46th are also known as "Murray's Bucks," "The Surprisers," and "The Doc's" (from the initials).

(*Depot*, Halifax.)
(*Record Office*, York.)
The Elephant, superscribed "Hindoostan."
"Dettingen," "Mysore," "Seringapatam," "Ally Ghur," "Delhi, 1803," "Leswarree," "Deig," "Corunna," "Nive," "Peninsula," "Waterloo," "Alma," "Inkerman," "Sevastopol," "Abyssinia," "Relief of Kimberley," "Paardeberg," "South Africa, 1900-02."
Motto: *Virtutis fortuna comes* (Fortune accompanies honour).
Uniform, Scarlet.
Facings, Scarlet.
Head-dress, Helmet.
Cap, Blue.
Regimental March, "The Wellesley."
The only regiment in the British Army named after a subject not of Royal blood.

THE DUKE OF WELLINGTON'S REGIMENT (West Riding)

Raised in 1702 as the 33rd Foot, and in 1814 nicknamed "The Havercake Lads," its recruiting sergeants preceding the recruits with a haver or oatcake stuck on their swords. From its earliest days the regiment was distinguished for bravery in the field, being commended in 1705-6 at the storming of Valentia d'Alcantara, and nearly annihilated at the battle of Almanza in 1707. The same bravery has marked it through the centuries, and to-day it is showing that its ancient courage is maintained undiminished. The Duke of Wellington served in it and afterwards commanded it, and the regiment was named after him.

The 2nd Battalion (76th Foot) became known in 1806 as "The Old Immortals," most of its men having been wounded or died in the ten or twelve years previously; "The Old Seven-and-Sixpennies," from its number; "The Hindoostan Regiment."

(*Depot*, Carlisle.)

(*Record Office*, Preston.)

A Laurel Wreath. The Dragon, superscribed "China."

"Havannah," "St. Lucia, 1778," "Albuhera," "Arroyo dos Molinos," "Vittoria," "Pyrenees," "Nivelle," "Nive," "Orthes," "Peninsula," "Alma," "Inkerman," "Sevastopol," "Lucknow," "Relief of Ladysmith," "South Africa, 1899-1902."

Uniform, Scarlet.

Facings, Yellow.

Head-dress, Helmet.

Cap, Blue.

Regimental March, "John Peel."

The laurel wreath borne on the colours is to commemorate its heroic conduct at the battle of Fontenoy, and is the only regiment to wear the honour "Arroyo dos Molinos."

THE BORDER REGIMENT

Raised in 1702. During the Peninsular War, at Arroyo dos Molinos it performed one of the most brilliant feats of the whole war; single handed the battalion cut off and made prisoners many French officers of distinction, besides an entire battalion of the French 34th of the Line, the brass drums and drum-major's staff of which are still in possession of the 1st Battalion. The 1st Battalion (34th Foot) was one of the "boy regiments" reformed in 1797 and sent to the Cape to be acclimatised. The 2nd Battalion (55th Foot) are known as "The Two Fives," from their number. The "Dragon" badge commemorates the services of the 55th in China, and it had the unique distinction for many years of wearing the red and white feather in their chacos, with red on top. Both battalions met in the Crimea, and did fine service before Sevastopol.

Nickname: "The Cattle Reeves," from the old traditions of the Scottish Border.

(*Depot*, Chichester.)

(*Record Office*, Hounslow.)

The White (Rousillon) Plume.

"Gibraltar, 1704-05," "Louisburg," "Quebec, 1759," "Martinique, 1762," "Havannah," "St. Lucia, 1778," "Maida," "Egypt, 1882," "Abu Klea," "Nile, 1884-85," "South Africa, 1900-02."

Uniform, Scarlet.

Facings, Blue.

Head-dress, Helmet.

Cap, Blue with Scarlet Band.

Regimental March, "The Royal Sussex."

The Badge of the Maltese Cross is in memory of the capture of Malta.

THE ROYAL SUSSEX REGIMENT

Raised in 1701. At Quebec, in 1759, in combat with the Grenadiers of the famous French regiment of Royal Rousillon, it won the tall white feather which was a distinguishing mark of the 35th until 1810. It is now commemorated in the Regimental Badge. It took part in the capture of Malta, where after the successful assault on Fort Ricasoli, the last post held by the French garrison, the King's Colour of the 35th was the first flag hoisted over the old stronghold of the Knights, destined thenceforward as an outpost of the British Empire. The 1st Battalion (35th Foot) was named "The Orange Lilies," from the colour of its facings, which it received as a mark of special favour from King William III. in 1701. It was called on its formation at Belfast "The Belfast Regiment," and afterwards "The Prince of Orange's Own Regiment," but its orange facings were relinquished and changed to blue in 1832, on the corps proceeding to Ireland. The 2nd Battalion (107th Foot) was raised in 1760 as the Queen's Own Royal British Volunteers.

(*Depot*, Winchester.)
(*Record Office*, Exeter.)
The Royal Tiger, superscribed "India."
"Blenheim," "Ramillies," "Oudenarde," "Malplaquet," "Dettingen," "Minden," "Tournay," "Barrosa," "Peninsula," "Taku Forts," "Pekin, 1860," "Charasiah," "Kabul, 1879," "Afghanistan, 1878-80," "Burma, 1885-87," "Paardeberg," "South Africa, 1900-02."
Uniform, Scarlet.
Facings, Yellow.
Head-dress, Helmet.
Cap, Blue.
Regimental March, "The Hampshire."
The 37th was the first British Regiment to march across India.

THE HAMPSHIRE REGIMENT

Raised in 1702, and within a year was in Holland, and bore a gallant part in Marlborough's campaigns. Few regiments can show a more eventful record of service during the whole of its career, and it has won fame in all parts of the world. The 37th is one of the six British infantry regiments which fought at the battle of Minden, 1st August, 1759; still commemorated in the regiment by the wearing of roses on the anniversary.

The 2nd Battalion (67th Foot) was raised in 1756 and after arduous service in the West Indies, the Peninsula, and elsewhere it went to India, where it served for twenty-one years and bore a distinguished part in the capture, after a siege of eleven days, of the fortress of Asseerghur, regarded as the Gibraltar of the East. For its gallantry in India the crest of the Royal Tiger was bestowed. In subsequent service in the East the 67th took part in the attack on the Taku Forts, where four Victoria Crosses were won by Hampshire men.

Nickname: "The Hampshire Tigers."

(*Depot*, Lichfield.)
(*Record Office*, Lichfield.)
The Sphinx, superscribed "Egypt."
"Guadaloupe, 1759," "Martinique, 1762," "Monte Video," "Roliça," "Vimiera," "Corunna," "Busaco," "Badajoz," "Salamanca," "Vittoria," "St. Sebastian," "Nive," "Peninsula," "Ava," "Moodkee," "Ferozeshah," "Sobraon," "Pegu," "Alma," "Inkerman," "Sevastopol," "Lucknow," "Central India," "South Africa, 1878-79," "Egypt, 1882," "Kirbekan," "Nile, 1884-85," "South Africa, 1900-02."
Uniform, Scarlet.
Facings, White.
Head-dress, Helmet.
Cap, Blue.
Regimental March, "Come, Lassies and Lads."

THE SOUTH STAFFORDSHIRE REGIMENT

Raised in 1702. In 1706, the 38th embarked for the West Indies, where it remained for nearly sixty years, most of the time in the island of Antigua. When the trouble arose in America, the 38th was one of the first regiments to be despatched thither and fought at Bunker's Hill. In 1805 it landed in South Africa and helped to re-capture the Cape of Good Hope from the Dutch. The 2nd Battalion has been shipwrecked no less than three times. On the first occasion when proceeding to take part in Abercromby's campaign in Egypt, when the mess-plate and all the regimental records were lost; again when returning to India on completion of the campaign; and again when proceeding to India from Australia in 1844. Lord Wolseley commenced his distinguished career in this regiment. The 1st Battalion (38th Foot) was called the "Pump and Tortoise," and the 2nd Battalion (80th Foot), the "Staffordshire Knots," and previously "The Staffordshire

Volunteers."

(*Depot*, Dorchester.)
(*Record Office*, Exeter.)
The Castle and Key, superscribed "Gibraltar, 1779-83."The Sphinx, superscribed "Egypt."
"Plassey," "Martinique, 1794," "Marabout," "Albuhera," "Vittoria," "Pyrenees," "Nivelle," "Nive," "Orthes," "Peninsula," "Ava," "Maharajpore," "Sevastopol," "Tirah," "Relief of Ladysmith," "South Africa, 1899-1902."
Motto: *Primus in Indis* (First in India).
Uniform, Scarlet.
Facings, Grass green.
Head-dress, Helmet.
Cap, Blue.
Regimental March, "The Dorsetshire."
The 1st Battalion is the proud possessor of a remarkable silver headed Drum-Major's Staff, which was presented to it by the Nawab of Arcot for its gallantry at the Battle of Plassey.

THE DORSETSHIRE REGIMENT

Raised in 1702, and was soon afterwards in action. The regiment was called "Sankey's Horse," because at the battle of Almanza, 1707, the men were mounted on mules to enable them to arrive in time for the battle. It was the first King's regiment landed in India in 1754, hence its proud legend *"Primus in Indis."* In 1742, from its "sad green" facings, it was christened the "Green Linnets."

The 2nd Battalion (54th Foot) was specially commended by the Commander-in-Chief for its remarkable gallantry and resolution when on board the "Sarah Sands" when that vessel took fire at sea having a large quantity of ammunition on board.

The 2nd Battalion derived the name of "Flamers" in 1781, from the part they took in destroying twelve privateers, and the town and stores of New London (U.S.), by fire. It also won for the regiment the proud crest of the Sphinx and the honour "Marabout" by great gallantry in Egypt in 1801.

(*Depot*, Warrington.)
(*Record Office*, Shrewsbury.)
The Sphinx, superscribed "Egypt."
"Louisburg," "Martinique, 1762," "Havannah," "St. Lucia, 1778," "Monte Video," "Roliça," "Vimiera," "Corunna," "Talavera," "Badajoz," "Salamanca," "Vittoria,"

"Pyrenees," "Nivelle," "Orthes," "Toulouse," "Peninsula," "Niagara," "Waterloo," "Candahar, 1842," "Ghuznee, 1842," "Cabool, 1842," "Maharajpore," "Sevastopol," "Lucknow," "New Zealand," "Relief of Ladysmith," "South Africa, 1899-1902."

Uniform, Scarlet.
Facings, White.
Head-dress, Helmet.
Cap, Blue.
Regimental March, "God Bless the Prince of Wales."
Allied Regiment, 9th (Wellington East Coast) Regiment of New Zealand.

PRINCE OF WALES'S VOLUNTEERS (South Lancashire Regiment)

The regiment (1st Battalion is the old 40th Foot) was raised in 1717, being formed from certain companies of infantry which for many years had been on duty in the West Indies, and remained for some 46 years longer in the West Indies and America, taking part in most of the historical military operations in that wonderful continent. On returning home the regiment was quickly on active service again on the Continent and in Egypt, and then had another spell of hard service in America, returning just in time to join Wellington's Army on the eve of Waterloo where they lost 25 killed and 142 wounded. The 1st Battalion has the proud distinction of being one of the three regiments which served uninterruptedly throughout the Peninsular War from 1808-1814. The 40th Foot was nicknamed "The Excellers," from its number XL., also "The Fighting Fortieth."

Private, 1756.
Drummer, 55th Regiment, 1792.
Grenadier, 55th Regiment, 1767.
The Border Regiment—The Colours.
British Infantry storming a village in modern warfare.

(*Depot*, Cardiff.)
(*Record Office*, Shrewsbury.)
A Naval Crown, superscribed "12th April, 1782."
"Martinique, 1762," "St. Vincent," "India," "Bourbon," "Java," "Detroit," "Queenstown," "Miami," "Niagara," "Waterloo," "Ava," "Candahar, 1842," "Ghuznee, 1842," "Cabool, 1842," "Alma," "Inkerman," "Sevastopol," "Relief of Kimberley," "Paardeberg," "South Africa, 1899-1902."

Motto: *Gwell angau na Chywilydd* (Death before Dishonour).
Uniform, Scarlet.
Facings, White.
Head-dress, Helmet.
Cap, Blue.
Regimental March, "Ap Shenkin."

THE WELSH REGIMENT

The 1st Battalion (41st Foot) was raised as a regiment of invalids in 1719, and it was for a long time known as the "1st Invalids," and as such appears in most of the old "Army Lists." In the era of George II., it distinguished itself in Germany.

The 2nd Battalion (the 69th Regiment) was known as "The Old Agamemnons," so called by Lord Nelson at the naval battle of St. Vincent, from the name of his ship, the "Agamemnon," on which the regiment served as Marines; also the "Ups and Downs" from the fact that their number can be read either way up.

The regiment has fought with the greatest distinction in many quarters of the world. The curious military arrangements which opened the door for abuse in bygone days are seen in the fact that Colonel Sir Henry Walton, K.C.B., who afterwards commanded the 23rd Regiment, received a commission on the day he was born, through the influence of his father, and at the age of four was gazetted Ensign in the 41st Foot on full pay, and at the age of thirteen was posted to the command of a company.

Nickname: "Wardour's Horse."

(*Depot*, Perth.)
(*Record Office*, Perth.)
The Sphinx, superscribed "Egypt."
"Guadaloupe, 1759," "Martinique, 1762," "Havannah," "North America, 1763-64," "Mangalore," "Mysore," "Seringapatam," "Corunna," "Busaco," "Fuentes d'Onor," "Pyrenees," "Nivelle," "Nive," "Orthes," "Toulouse," "Peninsula," "Waterloo," "South Africa, 1846-7, 1851-2-3," "Alma," "Sevastopol," "Lucknow," "Ashantee, 1873-4," "Tel-el-Kebir," "Egypt, 1882, 1884," "Kirbekan," "Nile, 1884-85," "Paardeberg," "South Africa, 1899-1902."

Motto: *Nemo me impune lacessit* (No one provokes me with impunity).
Uniform, Scarlet.
Facings, Blue.
Regimental Tartan.
Head-dress, Feather bonnet, scarlet, white and green diced border, scarlet hackle.

White sporran with five black tassels.
Blue glengarry cap.
Regimental March, "Highland Laddie."
The Pipers wear the feather bonnet the same as the men, being the only pipers to do so.
Allied Regiments:
5th Regiment "Royal Highlanders of Canada," and 1st Bn. New South Wales Scottish Rifle Regiment, Australia.

THE BLACK WATCH (Royal Highlanders)

The 1st Battalion (42nd Foot) was raised in 1730 from six independent companies of Highlanders for the protection of Edinburgh, as a regiment of the watch. In 1751, it was numbered the 42nd. On becoming amalgamated, the bright colours in the tartans were extracted, leaving only the dark green ground as a tartan, and from this circumstance rose the title "The Black Watch." In 1794, for gallant conduct at the battle of Guildermalsen, in Holland, it won the "red hackle" (or plume) which is worn in the men's feather bonnets.

Known as the "Forty-Twas."

(*Depot*, Oxford.)
(*Record Office*, Warwick.)
"Quebec, 1759," "Martinique, 1762," "Havannah," "Mysore," "Hindoostan," "Martinique, 1794," "Vimiera," "Corunna," "Busaco," "Fuentes d'Onor," "Ciudad Rodrigo," "Badajoz," "Salamanca," "Vittoria," "Pyrenees," "Nivelle," "Nive," "Orthes," "Toulouse," "Peninsula," "Waterloo," "South Africa, 1851-2-3," "Delhi, 1857," "New Zealand," "Relief of Kimberley," "Paardeberg," "South Africa, 1900-02."
Uniform, Scarlet.
Facings, White.
Head-dress, Helmet.
Cap, Green with green band.
Regimental March, "Nachtlager in Granada."
Allied Regiments, 52nd Regiment (Prince Albert Volunteers) of Canada and 6th (Hauraki) Regiment of New Zealand.
The Officers, alone among the infantry, have the privilege of wearing white strip collars with the frock coat.

THE OXFORDSHIRE & BUCKINGHAMSHIRE LIGHT

INFANTRY

Raised in 1741 and was dispatched almost at once on active service, serving at Minorca, Canada (taking part in the capture of Quebec), Martinique, and Havannah. The 43rd and 52nd, with the Rifle Brigade, made up the famous Light Infantry Brigade trained by Sir John Moore at Shorncliffe, and so laid the foundation for many famous victories in the Peninsula. The splendid service rendered by the Light Infantry in subsequent years is a matter of history. The regiment was so often chosen for leading the storming parties, that a badge "V.S." (Valiant Stormer) was granted to the men.

Nicknamed "The Light Bobs," a term that was applied generally to Light Infantry regiments.

(*Depot*, Warley.)
(*Record Office*, Warley.)
The Castle and Key, superscribed "Gibraltar, 1779-83."The Sphinx, superscribed "Egypt."An Eagle.
"Moro," "Havannah," "Badajoz," "Salamanca," "Peninsula," "Bladensburg," "Waterloo," "Ava," "Alma," "Inkerman," "Sevastopol," "Taku Forts," "Nile, 1884-85," "Relief of Kimberley," "Paardeberg," "South Africa, 1899-1902."
Uniform, Scarlet.
Facings, White.
Head-dress, Helmet.
Cap, Blue.
Regimental March, "The Essex."
At the Battle of Salamanca, 1812, the Eagle of the 62nd French regiment of the line was captured by the 44th. This trophy is now in the Chapel of Chelsea Hospital.

THE ESSEX REGIMENT

Raised in 1749 and during its long and eventful career has added lustre to the glory of the British Army. The 44th was the only British infantry regiment in Cabul, in the ill-fated 1841 campaign, and with all the native troops perished while attempting to reach Jellalabad. The story of the heroism of all ranks in that great disaster is a proud tradition in the regiment. The 1st Battalion (44th Foot) was known as the "Two Fours" from its number, also "The Little Fighting Fours." The 2nd Battalion (56th Foot) was nicknamed "The Pompadours," from the circumstance that, in 1755, when the regiment was raised, its facings were a crimson or puce colour, called in those days, Pompadour, after the notorious French lady who patronised it. It formed part of the gallant garrison of Gibraltar who successfully withstood the ten years' siege by the French and Spanish forces.

The Drums and Fifes.
A Review.—The March Past.

(*Depot*, Derby.)

(*Record Office*, Lichfield.)

"Louisburg," "Roliça," "Vimiera," "Talavera," "Busaco," "Fuentes d'Onor," "Ciudad Rodrigo," "Badajoz," "Salamanca," "Vittoria," "Pyrenees," "Nivelle," "Orthes," "Toulouse," "Peninsula," "Ava," "South Africa, 1846-7," "Alma," "Inkerman," "Sevastopol," "Central India," "Abyssinia," "Egypt, 1882," "Tirah," "South Africa, 1899-1902."

Uniform, Scarlet.

Facings, Lincoln green.

Head-dress, Helmet.

Cap, Blue.

Regimental March, "Young May Moon."

The tradition concerning the regimental march is that the regiment, in order to be present at the storming of Badajoz, set out on a long and arduous night march across some very rough country, the band playing "The Young May Moon," which the Colonel thereafter adopted as the regimented march.

THE SHERWOOD FORESTERS (Nottinghamshire and Derbyshire Regt.)

Raised in 1741, the regiment has rendered loyal service to King and country in all parts of the Empire, and has on more than one occasion received the thanks of General officers for their very fine fighting qualities. The 1st Battalion has the proud distinction of being one of the three regiments which served uninterruptedly throughout the Peninsular War from 1808 to 1814.

The 1st Battalion (45th Foot) was known as "The Old Stubborns" from their splendid bravery at the battle of Talavera, and "Sherwood Foresters," in reference to the traditions of the county of Nottingham. They claim descent from Robin Hood and his merry men.

(*Depot*, Preston.)

(*Record Office*, Preston.)

"Louisburg," "Quebec, 1759," "Maida," "Corunna," "Tarifa," "Vittoria," "St.

Sebastian," "Nive," "Peninsula," "Ava," "Alma," "Inkerman," "Sevastopol," "Ali Masjid," "Afghanistan, 1878-79," "Defence of Kimberley," "South Africa, 1899-02."

Uniform, Scarlet.

Facings, White.

Head-dress, Helmet.

Cap, Blue.

Regimental March, "The Red Rose."

THE LOYAL NORTH LANCASHIRE REGIMENT

This, the only Regular Infantry in the Army entitled to the word "Loyal" as part of their proud title, was raised in 1740 in Scotland, and was with Sir John Cope at Falkirk, and helped to defend Edinburgh Castle against the rebels in 1745. It afterwards went to America, was at the capture of Quebec, the capture of Martinique, and many other famous actions. The 2nd Battalion has added its quota to the splendid record standing to the credit of the Regiment, its work during the Indian Mutiny being specially brilliant.

The 1st Battalion (47th Foot) was nicknamed "The Cauliflowers," from their facings, and "The Lancashire Lads." It was known at Quebec as "Wolfe's Own," and wears a black line in the lace as an expression of sorrow for his death.

The 2nd Battalion (81st Foot) possessed a highly-prized title in that of the "Loyal Lincoln Volunteers."

(*Depot*, Northampton.)

(*Record Office*, Warley.)

The Castle and Key, superscribed "Gibraltar, 1779-83."The Sphinx, superscribed "Egypt."

"Louisburg," "Quebec, 1759," "Martinique, 1762," "Havannah," "Martinique, 1794," "Maida," "Douro," "Talavera," "Albuhera," "Badajoz," "Salamanca," "Vittoria," "Pyrenees," "Nivelle," "Orthes," "Toulouse," "Peninsula," "New Zealand," "Sevastopol," "South Africa, 1879," "Tirah," "Modder River," "South Africa, 1899-1902."

Uniform, Scarlet.

Facings, White.

Head-dress, Helmet.

Cap, Blue.

Regimental March, "The Northamptonshire."

Allied Regiment: 15th (North Auckland) Regiment of New Zealand.

THE NORTHAMPTONSHIRE REGIMENT

The two Battalions were raised in 1740 and 1755, and were brought together quite early in their careers, fighting side by side at Louisburg, at Quebec, and again at Salamanca, Vittoria, and in the Pyrenees. The regiment has seen active service in many parts of the world, and it is stated was the first to realise the value of modern musketry, through the bitter experience gained in the first Boer War. So impressed was the commanding officer by the terrible casualties suffered at the hands of the Boer marksmen, that he vowed he would make his battalion the best shooting unit in the Army, and after the war succeeded in so doing.

Nicknamed "The Steelbacks," so called from the unflinching manner in which the men took their floggings; also called "The Black Cuffs."

(*Depot*, Reading.)
(*Record Office*, Warwick.)
The Dragon, superscribed "China."
"St. Lucia, 1778," "Egmont-op-Zee," "Copenhagen," "Douro," "Talavera," "Albuhera," "Queenstown," "Vittoria," "Pyrenees," "Nivelle," "Nive," "Orthes," "Peninsula," "Alma," "Inkerman," "Sevastopol," "Kandahar, 1880," "Afghanistan, 1879-80," "Egypt, 1882," "Tofrek," "Suakin, 1885," "South Africa, 1899-1902."
Uniform, Scarlet.
Facings, Blue.
Head-dress, Helmet.
Cap, Blue, with scarlet band.
Regimental March, "Dashing White Sergeant."

PRINCESS CHARLOTTE OF WALES'S (Royal Berkshire Regiment)

The 1st Battalion (49th Foot) was raised in 1714, and had nearly eighty years West Indian and American service. On returning, the regiment was employed in subduing the mutiny in the Navy at the Nore, and then as Marines took part in the naval battle of Copenhagen. In 1803 the regiment again went to America, taking part in the operations against the United States. Active service in South Africa, China, and the Crimea added further to the good name of the regiment, the title "Royal" being bestowed for conspicuous gallantry at the action of Tofrek in the Sudan in 1885. The 2nd Battalion (66th Foot) was raised in 1755, and has an equally glorious record, being in 1814-16 reputed to be the finest and best disciplined regiment in Bengal. In the Afghan War the regiment fought at Maiwand, where their heroic stand, while suffering fearful losses, is remembered with pride in the Army.

The regiment is sometimes referred to as "The Biscuit Boys" on account of their depot being at Reading.

(*Depot*, Maidstone.)
(*Record Office*, Hounslow.)
The Sphinx, superscribed "Egypt."
"Vimiera," "Corunna," "Almaraz," "Vittoria," "Pyrenees," "Nive," "Orthes," "Peninsula," "Punniar," "Moodkee," "Ferozeshah," "Aliwal," "Sobraon," "Alma," "Inkerman," "Sevastopol," "Lucknow," "New Zealand," "Egypt, 1882," "Nile, 1884-85," "South Africa, 1900-02."
Motto:
Quo Fas et Gloria ducunt (Where Duty and Glory lead).
Uniform, Scarlet.
Facings, Blue.
Head-dress, Helmet.
Cap, Blue, with scarlet band.
Regimental March, "A Hundred Pipers."
Allied Regiment: 1st (Canterbury) Regiment of New Zealand.
The officers wear blue velvet facings, and on becoming a Royal Regiment, in 1831, it was specially authorised to adhere to the velvet for its officers' facings.

THE QUEEN'S OWN (Royal West Kent Regiment)

Raised in 1755, and given black facings, which were retained till the "Royal" title was bestowed in 1831. No regiment has a more honourable record of service. The brunt of the battle of Corunna fell on the 50th, whom Sir John Moore congratulated during the battle, calling out "Well done, 50th! well done!"

Nicknames: "The Blind Half-Hundred," and "The Dirty Half-Hundred," from the men in action and in "*sweating*" weather wiping their faces with their black cuffs; also "The Devil's Royals." During the war in Spain, at the battle of Vimiera, 1807, the 50th completely routed the enemy, and received the title of "The Gallant Fiftieth."

The 2nd Battalion (97th Foot) nicknamed "The Celestials," from its former sky-blue facings.

(*Depot*, Pontefract.)
(*Record Office*, York.)

"Minden," "Corunna," "Fuentes d'Onor," "Salamanca," "Vittoria," "Pyrenees," "Nivelle," "Orthes," "Peninsula," "Waterloo," "Pegu," "Ali Masjid," "Afghanistan, 1878-80," "Burma, 1885-87," "Modder River," "South Africa, 1899-1902."

Motto: *Cede nullis* (Yield to none).

Uniform, Scarlet.

Facings, Blue.

Head-dress, Helmet.

Cap, Dark green.

Regimental March, "Jockey to the Fair."

Allied Regiment, 105th Regiment (Saskatoon Fusiliers) of Canada.

THE KING'S OWN (Yorkshire Light Infantry)

The 1st Battalion (51st Foot) was raised in 1756 and was "Yorkshire" from its birth, being intimately connected with the West Riding. It performed gallant service in all parts of the world, reaping with the 2nd Battalion (105th Foot), raised in 1839, a rich harvest of "honours," all of which, however, do not figure on the colours. Sir John Moore served as an ensign and a field officer in the regiment, and it came under his command in the famous retreat to Corunna, during which the Light Division rendered signal service in the rear guard. The 2nd Battalion was originally a regiment in the pay of the East India Company, and came to England for the first time in 1874.

Nickname: The "Kolis," that word being formed of the initial letters of the words which composed their regimental title—King's Own Light Infantry.

(*Depot*, Shrewsbury.)

(*Record Office*, Shrewsbury.)

"Nieuport," "Tournay," "St. Lucia, 1796," "Talavera," "Fuentes d'Onor," "Salamanca," "Vittoria," "Pyrenees," "Nivelle," "Nive," "Toulouse," "Peninsula," "Bladensburg," "Aliwal," "Sobraon," "Goojerat," "Punjaub," "Lucknow," "Afghanistan, 1879-80," "Egypt, 1882," "Suakin, 1885," "Paardeberg," "South Africa, 1899-1902."

Motto: *Aucto splendore resurgo* (I rise with increased splendour).

Uniform, Scarlet.

Facings, Blue.

Head-dress, Helmet.

Cap, Dark green, with green band.

Regimental March, "Old Towler."

THE KING'S (Shropshire Light Infantry)

Raised in 1755. This regiment is the only one to bear the honour "Nieuport," on its colours, winning this in 1793 by gallantly defending that town against a surprise attack by the enemy. At Tournay the regiment, with the 14th and 37th, by a forced march reached the battlefield at a most opportune moment and decided the day in favour of the British. The regiment was in St. Helena during the time Napoleon was held captive there, and that great soldier spoke frequently in tones of high praise of its conduct. It has maintained that good name throughout its subsequent career.

Nicknames: The 1st Battalion (53rd Foot)—"The Brickdusts," from their facings, which were red at one time; also "Old Five and Threepennies," from its number. The 2nd Battalion (85th Foot)—"Elegant Extracts," it being reformed with officers picked from other regiments.

(*Depot*, Mill Hill.)
(*Record Office*, Hounslow.)
"Mysore," "Seringapatam," "Albuhera," "Ciudad Rodrigo," "Badajoz," "Vittoria," "Pyrenees," "Nivelle," "Nive," "Peninsula," "Alma," "Inkerman," "Sevastopol," "New Zealand," "South Africa, 1879," "Relief of Ladysmith," "South Africa, 1900-02."
Uniform, Scarlet.
Facings, Lemon yellow.
Head-dress, Helmet.
Cap, Blue.
Regimental Marches, 1st and 3rd Battns., "Sir Manley Power"; 2nd and 4th Battns., "Paddy's Resource."
Allied Regiments, 57th Regiment (Peterborough Rangers) of Canada; 77th Wentworth Regiment of Canada; and 11th Regiment (Taranaki Rifles) of New Zealand.

THE DUKE OF CAMBRIDGE'S OWN (Middlesex Regiment)

Raised in 1755 chiefly of Londoners from the Middlesex Militia, and nicknamed the "Steelbacks," from being frequently flogged by the provost. From their extraordinary fighting propensities at Albuhera, they earned the more honourable and famous name of the "Die-Hards." In this action, out of 25 officers, they had 22 killed and wounded; of 570 rank and file, killed and wounded 425. The King's colour was riddled by thirty bullets; Inglis, the heroic colonel, cried out frequently: "Die hard, my men, die hard," and from that day the gallant 57th were recognised in camp and barrack as the "Die-Hards." At Inkerman the officer commanding the 57th inspired his followers at a critical moment by the thrilling words, "Die-hards, remember Albuhera." The 2nd Battalion (77th Foot) was called "The Pot-hooks," from the figure 7, and was one of the three regiments which stormed the breach at Ciudad Rodrigo.

The Glorious Gallantry of the Regiment at Albuhera.
The Manchester Regiment.
Commanding Officer, Adjutant & Sergeant-Major.

(*Depot*, Winchester.)

(*Record Office*, Winchester.)

"Louisburg," "Quebec, 1759," "Martinique, 1762," "Havannah," "North America, 1763-64," "Roliça," "Vimiera," "Martinique, 1809," "Talavera," "Busaco," "Fuentes d'Onor," "Albuhera," "Ciudad Rodrigo," "Badajoz," "Salamanca," "Vittoria," "Pyrenees," "Nivelle," "Nive," "Orthes," "Toulouse," "Peninsula," "Mooltan," "Goojerat," "Punjaub," "South Africa, 1851-2-3," "Delhi, 1857," "Taku Forts," "Pekin, 1860," "South Africa, 1879," "Ahmad Khel," "Kandahar, 1880," "Afghanistan, 1878-80," "Tel-el-Kebir," "Egypt, 1882, 1884," "Chitral," "Defence of Ladysmith," "Relief of Ladysmith," "South Africa, 1899-1902."

Motto: *Celer et Audax* (Alert and Intrepid).

Uniform, Green.

Facings, Scarlet.

Head-dress, Busby, with black plume, with scarlet base.

Cap, Green, with green band.

Regimental March, "The Wild Hunt."

Allied Regiments, 60th Rifles of Canada; 63rd Regiment "Halifax Rifles," of Canada.

KING'S ROYAL RIFLE CORPS

The regiment was raised in New York in 1755. The uniform was scarlet with blue facings. It became the first green-coated rifle regiment in 1797, having scarlet facings and black leathern helmets. The roll of honour shows how well the regiment has served in all the subsequent campaigns, and it has a reputation for bravery and discipline second to none in the Army.

Nicknames: "The Greenjackets," from the colour of the uniform; "The Jaegers"; "The 60th Rifles"; and quite recently has been jocularly dubbed "The Kaiser's Own" from the fact that the regimental badge, a Maltese Cross, closely resembles the Iron Cross.

(*Depot*, Devizes.)

(*Record Office*, Exeter.)
"Louisburg," "Nive," "Peninsula," "New Zealand," "Ferozeshah," "Sobraon," "Sevastopol," "Pekin, 1860," "South Africa, 1879, 1900-02."
Uniform, Scarlet.
Facings, Buff.
Head-dress, Helmet.
Cap, Blue.
Regimental March, "The Wiltshire."
Allied Regiment: 10th (North Otago) Regiment of New Zealand.

THE DUKE OF EDINBURGH'S (Wiltshire Regiment)

The 1st Battalion (62nd Foot) was raised in 1756 as the 2nd Battalion of the King's Own, and was soon afterwards formed as a separate corps. It quickly gained a name for itself when four companies made a gallant stand among the ruins of Carrick Fergus Castle against a thousand French troops with artillery, the 62nd maintaining their defence with bricks and stones after their ammunition was exhausted, and had even fired away their buttons as bullets. Their gallant conduct was commemorated by wearing a "splash" on their buttons for many years afterwards. In 1831 while on service in India, cholera carried off nearly the whole regiment, there being at one time only two men not on the sick list or in hospital. The 2nd Battalion (99th Foot) was raised in 1824. Both battalions have splendid records of war service.

Nicknamed: "The Springers," from the rapidity of its pursuit of the American rebels after the action at Trois Rivieres, in Canada, 1776; also "The Splashers" and "The Moonrakers."

(*Depot*, Ashton-under-Lyne.)
(*Record Office*, Preston.)
The Sphinx, superscribed "Egypt."
"Guadaloupe, 1759," "Egmont-op-Zee," "Peninsula," "Martinique, 1809," "Guadaloupe, 1810," "New Zealand," "Alma," "Inkerman," "Sevastopol," "Afghanistan, 1879-80," "Egypt, 1882," "Defence of Ladysmith," "South Africa, 1899-1902."
Uniform, Scarlet.
Facings, White.
Head-dress, Helmet.
Cap, Blue.
Regimental March, "The Manchesters."

Allied Regiment: 8th (Southland) Regiment of New Zealand.

THE MANCHESTER REGIMENT

The 1st Battalion was raised in 1758, and after a brief spell of service on the Continent went to the West Indies and America, winning high praise for gallant conduct at the battle of Entaw. For very many years the regiment did splendid service in the West Indies, adding much territory to the British Empire, and was afterwards sent to Australia and New Zealand. Excellent service was rendered in the Crimea, India, and Afghanistan, the "Regimental Order of Merit" being founded with power to grant medals or badges, for specially gallant conduct. The regiment has served with honour in all parts of the Empire.

The Officers of the 63rd previous to 1855 wore a *fleur-de-lis* in gold embroidery at the end of their coat-tails. At one time the whole regiment appears to have worn a *fleur-de-lis* badge, which was adopted in 1815 for services rendered at Guadaloupe.

The 1st Battalion (63rd Foot) nicknamed "Bloodsuckers," at one time. The 2nd Battalion (96th Foot) was called "The Bendovers."

(*Depot*, Lichfield.)
(*Record Office*, Lichfield.)
The Dragon, superscribed "China."
"Guadaloupe, 1759," "Martinique, 1794," "St. Lucia, 1803," "Surinam," "Punjaub," "Reshire," "Bushire," "Koosh-ab," "Persia," "Lucknow," "Hafir," "South Africa, 1900-02."
Uniform, Scarlet.
Facings, White.
Head-dress, Helmet.
Cap, Blue.
Regimental March, "The days when we went gipsying."

THE PRINCE OF WALES'S (North Staffordshire Regiment)

The 1st Battalion (64th Foot) was raised in 1756, the facings being black. It took part in the hardest fighting in the West Indies and America, being engaged there off and on till 1815, reaching home just too late to take part in the battle of Waterloo. The regiment was on board the "Alert," when she was wrecked near Halifax, N.S., all ranks remaining below silent and under perfect discipline, while the vessel was run ashore. Had the men attempted to reach the deck the vessel would have foundered. By their discipline everyone aboard was saved, and the Duke of Wellington ordered that the details should be published throughout the Army as an example of discipline. The 2nd Battalion (98th Foot) was raised in 1824 and served in the Crimean War. The 98th was honoured with the title of "Prince of Wales's" in recognition of the duties performed by the Corps during the Prince of Wales's visit to Malta.

Nicknamed: "The Black Knots" as distinct from "The Staffordshire Knots" of the South Staffordshire Regiment.

(*Depot*, Pontefract.)
(*Record Office*, York.)
The Royal Tiger, superscribed "India."
"Guadaloupe, 1759," "Martinique, 1794," "India, 1796-1819," "Nive," "Peninsula," "Arabia," "New Zealand," "Lucknow," "Tel-el-Kebir," "Egypt, 1882, 1884," "Relief of Ladysmith," "South Africa, 1899-1902."
Uniform, Scarlet.
Facings, White.
Head-dress, Helmet.
Cap, Blue.
Regimental March, "The York and Lancaster."
Allied Regiment: 5th (Wellington) Regiment of New Zealand.

YORK & LANCASTER REGIMENT

Raised in 1756 and was present at the capture of Guadaloupe. Active service in the West Indies reduced the ranks to such an extent that on its return it had to take large drafts of "parish boys." In 1801 the "boy" regiment was sent to the Cape to get acclimatised for service in India, where it arrived two years later, and where it stayed for over twenty years earning a high reputation for bravery and discipline. Later, another long spell of foreign service was put in, serving for no fewer than twenty years in Australia and New Zealand, a unique experience. The 2nd Battalion was raised as the 84th Foot in 1793 at York, and saw a great deal of foreign and active service, part being among the small garrison of Lucknow during the Mutiny, the rest of the 84th being massacred at Cawnpore. The brilliant record of service of the regiment has been added to since those days.

Nickname: "The Royal Tigers" and "The Twin Roses."

(*Depot*, Newcastle.)
(*Record Office*, York.)

"Salamanca," "Vittoria," "Pyrenees," "Nivelle," "Orthes," "Peninsula," "Alma," "Inkerman," "Sevastopol," "Reshire," "Bushire," "Koosh-ab," "Persia," "New Zealand," "Relief of Ladysmith," "South Africa, 1899-1902."

Uniform, Scarlet.

Facings, Dark green.

Head-dress, Helmet.

Cap, Green with green band.

Regimental March, "The Light Barque."

Allied Regiments, 106th Regiment (Winnipeg Light Infantry) of Canada; 2nd (South Canterbury) Regiment of New Zealand.

THE DURHAM LIGHT INFANTRY

No regiment has earned a prouder title than the Durhams, that of "The Faithful Durhams" having been bestowed for devoted service on many a hard won battlefield and for years of arduous service faithfully performed. The 1st Battalion (68th Foot) was raised in 1756 by General John Lambton of the Coldstream Guards, and was soon on active service on the Continent, followed by active service in the West Indies. For nine years, the 68th garrisoned Gibraltar, and afterwards took part in the capture of St. Lucia, 1795, and St. Vincent. In the Peninsula, it added to its already high reputation, which it has since so well enhanced on the Continent. The 2nd Battalion (106th Foot) was raised in India in 1826 by the East India Company as the 2nd Bombay European Regiment, serving with credit in many actions in India and Persia, coming to England for the first time in 1871.

Nickname: "The Faithful Durhams."

(*Depot*, Hamilton.)

(*Record Office*, Hamilton.)

The Castle and Key, superscribed "Gibraltar, 1780-83."The Elephant, superscribed "Assaye."

"Carnatic," "Hindoostan," "Sholinghur," "Mysore," "Seringapatam," "Cape of Good Hope, 1806," "Roliça," "Vimiera," "Corunna," "Busaco," "Fuentes d'Onor," "Ciudad Rodrigo," "Badajoz," "Almaraz," "Salamanca," "Vittoria," "Pyrenees," "Nivelle," "Nive," "Orthes," "Toulouse," "Peninsula," "Waterloo," "South Africa, 1851-2-3," "Sevastopol," "Central India," "Tel-el-Kebir," "Egypt, 1882," "Modder River," "South Africa, 1899-1902."

Uniform, Scarlet doublet with Mackenzie tartan trews.

Facings, Buff.

Head-dress, Blue chaco with green tuft and crimson, white and green diced border. Band, Feather bonnet with green, crimson and white diced border, and scarlet hackle.
Cap, Green Glengarry.
Regimental March, "Whistle o'er the lave o't."

HIGHLAND LIGHT INFANTRY

The regiment has one of the most brilliant records in the whole army, a reputation it splendidly maintained against the Germans in France and Belgium. The 1st Battalion (71st Foot) dates from 1777 as Fraser's Highlanders, which afterwards became Macleod's Highlanders, fighting with distinguished bravery in India, South Africa, the Peninsula, Waterloo and elsewhere. The 2nd Battalion (74th Foot) has an equally brilliant record of Indian and foreign service, winning great glory at the battle of Assaye, where every officer was killed or wounded and the remainder of the regiment was brought out of action by the Sergeant-Major.

The 1st Battalion was so full of Glasgow men during the Peninsular War, that it was generally known as "The Glesca Keelies."

(*Depot*, Fort George.)
(*Record Office*, Perth.)
The Elephant, superscribed "Assaye."
"Carnatic," "Hindoostan," "Mysore," "Cape of Good Hope, 1806," "Maida," "Java," "South Africa, 1835," "Sevastopol," "Koosh-ab," "Persia," "Lucknow," "Central India," "Peiwar Kotal," "Charasiah," "Kabul, 1879," "Kandahar, 1880," "Afghanistan, 1878-80," "Tel-el-Kebir," "Egypt, 1882," "Chitral," "Atbara," "Khartoum," "Paardeberg," "South Africa, 1899-1902."

Mottoes: *Cuidich'n Righ* (Help, to the King); *Caber Feidh* (Antlers of the Deer), the war cry of Seaforth; *Tulloch Ard* (The high Hill), the slogan of Kintail.
Uniform, Scarlet.
Facings, Buff.
Mackenzie tartan.
White sporran with two black tails.
Head-dress, Feather bonnet, scarlet, white and green diced border; white hackle, except bandsmen who wear scarlet.
Cap, Glengarry, with scarlet, white and green diced border.
Regimental March, "Highland Laddie."
Allied Regiments, 72nd Regiment (Seaforth Highlanders of Canada); 78th Pictou Regiment (Highlanders) of Canada.

SEAFORTH HIGHLANDERS (Rossshire Buffs, the Duke of Albany's)

The 1st Battalion (72nd Highlanders) was raised by the chief of the Clan Mackenzie in 1778. The regiment gave early evidence of that great bravery which has ever marked it, especially in India and Afghanistan, and took part in the whole of the Egyptian and Soudan expeditions from the attack at Tel-el-Kebir to the final battle at Omdurman. The 2nd Battalion (78th Highlanders) claim descent from the famous Fraser Highlanders of 1756, being reorganized at Aberdeen in 1793 as the Rossshire Buffs and has an equally glorious record.

Nickname: 1st Battalion, "The Macraes"; 2nd Battalion, "King's Men," from the motto.

Argyll & Sutherland Highlanders—Officers in Review Order.
Gordon Highlanders.—Officers in Review Order.

(*Depot*, Aberdeen.)
(*Record Office*, Perth.)

The Royal Tiger, superscribed "India."The Sphinx, superscribed "Egypt."

"Mysore," "Seringapatam," "Egmont-op-Zee," "Mandora," "Corunna," "Fuentes d'Onor," "Almaraz," "Vittoria," "Pyrenees," "Nive," "Orthes," "Peninsula," "Waterloo," "South Africa, 1835," "Delhi, 1857," "Lucknow," "Charasiah," "Kabul, 1879," "Kandahar, 1880," "Afghanistan, 1878-80," "Tel-el-Kebir," "Egypt, 1882, 1884," "Nile, 1884-85," "Chitral," "Tirah," "Defence of Ladysmith," "Paardeberg." "South Africa, 1899-1902."

Motto: *Bydand* (Watchful).
Uniform, Scarlet.
Facings, Yellow.
Gordon tartan with yellow stripe.
White sporran with two black tails.
Head-dress, Feather bonnet, scarlet, white and green diced border with white hackle.
Cap, Glengarry, with scarlet, white and green diced border.
Regimental March, "Highland Laddie."
Allied Regiment, 48th Regiment (Highlanders) of Canada.

THE GORDON HIGHLANDERS

"The Gay Gordons," as the regiment has always been known, are the lineal descendants of that famous regiment raised in 1787, mainly by the beautiful Duchess of Gordon, who bestowed on each recruit a kiss. The regiment saw a great deal of service in India, notably the storming of Seringapatam. Service in the Mediterranean and South Africa followed, and the regiment was back in India in time to take part in some of the severest fighting in the Mutiny. Brilliant service in other parts of the Empire followed. The 2nd Battalion (92nd Highlanders) trace their history back to 1794, and fought in India, the Peninsula and at Waterloo with great credit. Many famous officers have commenced their military careers in the Gordon Highlanders.

(*Depot*, Inverness.)
(*Record Office*, Perth.)
The Sphinx, superscribed "Egypt."
"Egmont-op-Zee," "Corunna," "Busaco," "Fuentes d'Onor," "Salamanca," "Pyrenees," "Nivelle," "Nive," "Toulouse," "Peninsula," "Waterloo," "Alma," "Sevastopol," "Lucknow," "Tel-el-Kebir," "Egypt, 1882," "Nile, 1884-85," "Atbara," "Khartoum," "South Africa, 1900-02."
Uniform, Scarlet.
Facings, Blue. *Tartan*, Cameron-Erracht.
Black sporran, with two white tails.
Head-dress, Feather bonnet, scarlet, white and green diced border and white hackle.
Cap, Blue glengarry.
Regimental March, "Highland Laddie."
Allied Regiment: 79th Cameron Highlanders of Canada.

THE QUEEN'S OWN CAMERON HIGHLANDERS

The regiment (79th Foot) was raised by Cameron of Erracht in 1793 in Inverness-shire almost entirely from among his own kinsmen, and down to the present day the Clan Cameron is still very strong in the regiment. For many years the 79th Highlanders was the only single battalion regiment in the army, the 2nd Battalion being raised during the South African War. A remarkable fact in connection with the regiment was that although they had over 700 officers and men down with typhus on returning from Corunna in 1809, they did not lose a single man, and six months later embarked for the ill-fated Walcheren expedition 1,002 strong. They served in the trenches throughout the whole of that campaign without losing a man.

(*Depot*, Belfast.)
(*Record Office*, Dublin.)
The Sphinx, superscribed "Egypt."
"India," "Cape of Good Hope, 1806," "Talavera," "Bourbon," "Busaco," "Fuentes

d'Onor," "Ciudad Rodrigo," "Badajoz," "Salamanca," "Vittoria," "Nivelle," "Orthes," "Toulouse," "Peninsula," "Central India," "South Africa, 1899-1902."

Motto: Quis separabit? (Who shall separate?)
Uniform, Green.
Facings, Dark Green.
Head-dress, Black fur busby, with black and green plume.
Cap, Green with green band.
Regimental March, "Off, Off, said the Stranger."

THE ROYAL IRISH RIFLES

The regiment was raised in 1793 in Dublin by Col. Fitch, and became known as "Fitch's Grenadiers," the title being bestowed in humorous allusion to the small stature of the men. They, however, soon showed they could fight as well as the finest grenadiers in the Army, reaping glory in many a hot engagement during the succeeding years. The regiment was converted into Rifles in 1881 when the 86th Foot was linked with the 83rd as sister battalion. The 86th regiment was raised in 1792, as the Royal County Downs, and served for some years as marines, and later in Egypt. During the ten succeeding years the regiment travelled twice round Africa, served in India and the Red Sea, twice crossed the Egyptian Desert, served in South Africa, Ceylon, and elsewhere, the service being so strenuous that during five years in India over a thousand men laid down their lives. The fine physique of the ranks earned for them the name of the "Irish Giants."

(*Depot*, Armagh.)
(*Record Office*, Dublin.)
The Sphinx, superscribed "Egypt."
"Monte Video," "Talavera," "Barrosa," "Java," "Tarifa," "Vittoria," "Nivelle," "Niagara," "Orthes," "Toulouse," "Peninsula," "Ava," "Sevastopol," "Tel-el-Kebir," "Egypt, 1882, 1884," "Relief of Ladysmith," "South Africa, 1899-1902."

Motto: Faugh-a-Ballagh (Clear the way).
Uniform, Scarlet.
Facings, Blue.
Head-dress, Racoon-skin cap with green plume on left side.
Cap, Blue with scarlet band.
Regimental March, "British Grenadiers."

PRINCESS VICTORIA'S (Royal Irish Fusiliers)

The 1st Battalion (87th Foot) was raised by General Doyle in Ireland in 1793 and was fighting in 1794 in Belgium and afterwards saw a great deal of rough service in South America. It was, however, in the Peninsular War that it earned undying fame, charging the enemy who were in greatly superior numbers, at Barrosa, with such fury as to overthrow them, and led to the capture of an eagle by Sergt. Patrick Masterman, whose grandson won a V.C. in South Africa. In recognition of its splendid bravery the regiment was given a Royal title and directed to display an eagle as badge. The regiment has exhibited the same high standard of bravery in all its subsequent campaigns. The 2nd Battalion (89th Foot), raised in 1793, also made a splendid name for courage.

Nicknames: 1st Battalion, "The Old Fogs," or the "Faugh-a-Ballagh Boys"; 2nd Battalion, "The Rollickers."

(*Depot*, Galway.)
(*Record Office*, Cork.)
The Elephant.
The Sphinx, superscribed "Egypt."
"Seringapatam," "Talavera," "Busaco," "Fuentes d'Onor," "Ciudad Rodrigo," "Badajoz," "Salamanca," "Vittoria," "Pyrenees," "Nivelle," "Orthes," "Toulouse," "Peninsula," "Alma," "Inkerman," "Sevastopol," "Central India," "South Africa, 1877-8-9," "Relief of Ladysmith," "South Africa, 1899-1902."
Motto: *Quis separabit?* (Who shall separate?)
Uniform, Scarlet.
Facings, Green.
Head-dress, Helmet.
Cap, Blue with dark green band.
Regimental March, "St. Patrick's Day."

THE CONNAUGHT RANGERS

The 1st Battalion (88th Foot) dates from 1793, being raised in Connaught, and was known then by the same title it still bears. It has had a most adventurous career, being shipwrecked and seeing hard service in India, Egypt, Ceylon, and South America, and subsequently joining Wellington in the Peninsula, winning high distinction in many battles, especially at the sieges of Ciudad Rodrigo and Badajos. In 1819 the regiment was given permission to create a regimental order of merit, the 1st class being for those who had been in twelve or more general actions, and no fewer than 70 rank and file then serving qualified, there being nearly 130 who had been in from six to eleven actions, and over four hundred who had served in one to five actions. The 2nd Battalion (94th Foot) dates from 1823.

Nickname: "The Devil's Own," called so by General Picton for their undaunted bravery in face of the enemy; also "The Garvies."

(*Depot*, Stirling.)
(*Record Office*, Perth.)
"Cape of Good Hope, 1806," "Roliça," "Vimiera," "Corunna," "Pyrenees," "Nivelle," "Nive," "Orthes," "Toulouse," "Peninsula," "South Africa, 1846-7, 1851-2-3," "Alma," "Balaklava," "Sevastopol," "Lucknow," "South Africa, 1879," "Modder River," "Paardeberg," "South Africa, 1899-1902."
Mottoes: *Ne obliviscaris* (Forget not); *Sans Peur* (Without fear).
Uniform, Scarlet.
Facings, Yellow.
Tartan, Sutherland.
Black sporran, with six white tassels.
Head-dress, Feather bonnet, white hackle.
Cap, Glengarry with scarlet and white diced border.
Regimental March, "Highland Laddie."
Allied Regiment: 91st Regt. (Canadian Highlanders) of Canada.

PRINCESS LOUISE'S (Argyll and Sutherland Highlanders)

The 98th Highlanders (Argyllshire) was raised in 1796 and renumbered the 91st Highlanders in 1802, its constant war service being in South Africa where it helped to capture the Cape of Good Hope from the Dutch and took part in the first Kaffir War. It afterwards went to the Peninsula and fought in many of the battles there, winning great fame. Afterwards it served many years in the Mediterranean and in India, taking a full share in the fierce battles of the Mutiny. The 2nd Battalion, raised in 1800 as the Sutherland Highlanders, won its greatest glory in the Crimea where in line, under the brave Colin Campbell, it received unsupported the full charge of the Russian Cavalry and drove them off in confusion.

Known after the Battle of Balaklava as "The Thin Red Line," also called "The Rory's."

(*Depot*, Birr.)
(*Record Office*, Cork.)

"Niagara,"
"Central India,"
"South Africa, 1900-02."
Uniform, Scarlet.
Facings, Blue.
Head-dress, Helmet.
Cap, Blue with scarlet band.
Regimental March, "The Royal Canadian."
Allied Regiments: 10th Regiment (Royal Grenadiers) of Canada; 100th Winnipeg Grenadiers of Canada.

THE PRINCE OF WALES'S LEINSTER REGIMENT
(Royal Canadians)

The Leinster Regiment is the only British corps having a Colonial title. The 1st Battalion (100th Foot) was raised in Canada in 1858, and has, by marked gallantry in India, South Africa and Belgium, added much to the glory of the British Army. The 2nd Battalion (109th Foot) was raised in India in 1853. The regiment has many curious nicknames, those applying to the 1st Battalion being "The Crusaders," "The Centipedes," on account of its regimental number, the 100th, "The Beavers," the "Old Hundredth," and "The Colonials." At one time the colours used to be decorated with maple leaves on July 1st (Dominion Day), the maple leaf being borne as part of the badge. The 2nd Battalion is known as "The Poonah Pets" from its birthplace; "The Steel Heads" on account of withstanding the excessive heat of the sun in Central India, and "The Lilywhites" from its white facings. The regiment was the last British infantry unit to be quartered in Canada, and the whole country parted with them with regret.

(*Depot*, Tralee.)
(*Record Office*, Cork.)
A Royal Tiger.
"Plassey," "Condore," "Masulipatam," "Badara," "Buxar," "Rohilcund, 1774," "Sholinghur," "Carnatic," "Rohilcund, 1794," "Guzerat," "Deig," "Bhurtpore," "Ghuznee, 1839," "Affghanistan, 1839," "Ferozeshah," "Sobraon," "Chillianwallah," "Goojerat," "Punjaub," "Pegu," "Delhi, 1857," "Lucknow," "Burma, 1885-87," "South Africa, 1899-1902."
Uniform, Scarlet.
Facings, Blue.

Head-dress, Racoon-skin cap with white and green plume on left side.
Cap, Blue, with scarlet band.
Regimental March, "British Grenadiers."
Allied Regiments, 101st Regiment (Edmonton Fusiliers) of Canada; 104th Regiment (Westminster Fusiliers) of Canada.

THE ROYAL MUNSTER FUSILIERS

The 101st and 104th Regiments, combined to make up the Royal Munster Fusiliers, are both of Indian origin and have left their names deeply inscribed on the battles which gave that country to the Empire. The 101st was raised by Clive in India in 1756 as the Bengal European Regiment and shared in all the hard fighting from Chandernagore to Burmah, till the Mutiny brought them their crowning glory. After over one hundred years' campaigning the regiment came to England for the first time in 1868. The 2nd Battalion (the 104th Regiment) was formed in 1839 in Bengal and also did splendid service in the Mutiny and in the Burmah campaign.

Nickname: "The Dirty Shirts," a cherished name given them as a result of fighting in their shirt sleeves at Delhi, in 1857.

Army Service Corps.—A Field Bakery.
Royal Dublin Fusiliers—Officers with Colours.

(*Depot*, Naas.)
(*Record Office*, Dublin.)
The Royal Tiger, superscribed "Plassey," "Buxar."The Elephant, superscribed "Carnatic," "Mysore."
"Arcot," "Condore," "Wandiwash," "Pondicherry," "Guzerat," "Sholinghur," "Nundy Droog," "Amboyna," "Ternate," "Banda," "Seringapatam," "Kirkee," "Maheidpoor," "Beni Boo Alli," "Ava," "Aden," "Mooltan," "Goojerat," "Punjaub," "Pegu," "Lucknow," "Relief of Ladysmith," "South Africa, 1899-1902."
Motto: *Spectamur Agendo* (We are judged by our deeds).
Uniform, Scarlet.
Facings, Blue.
Head-dress, Racoon-skin cap, with blue and green plume on left side.
Cap, Bright blue, with scarlet band.
Regimental March, "British Grenadiers."

THE ROYAL DUBLIN FUSILIERS

The regiment is the oldest of the old Indian regiments. It was raised in India in the reign of Charles I., but in 1748 it became the Madras European Regiment, and under Clive rendered splendid service at many famous Indian battles which gradually won that Empire for the British Crown. The 2nd Battalion (103rd Foot) has an equally glorious Indian record. After 223 years of Indian service the 1st Battalion came to England for the first time in 1868, and in 1870 the 2nd Battalion came home for the first time after 209 years service.

Nicknames: "The Blue Caps." During the Indian Mutiny, Nana Sahib warned his men against those "blue-capped soldiers who fought like devils." "The Old Toughs," from the long period of hard service in India.

(*Depot*, Winchester.)
(*Record Office*, Winchester.)
"Copenhagen," "Monte Video," "Roliça," "Vimiera," "Corunna," "Busaco," "Barrosa," "Fuentes d'Onor," "Ciudad Rodrigo," "Badajoz," "Salamanca," "Vittoria," "Pyrenees," "Nivelle," "Nive," "Orthes," "Toulouse," "Peninsula," "Waterloo," "South Africa, 1846-7, 1851-2-3," "Alma," "Inkerman," "Sevastopol," "Lucknow," "Ashantee, 1873-4," "Ali Masjid," "Afghanistan, 1878-9," "Burma, 1885-87," "Khartoum," "Defence of Ladysmith," "Relief of Ladysmith," "South Africa, 1899-1902."
Uniform, Dark Green.
Facings, Black.
Head-dress, Black fur busby with black plume.
Cap, Dark Green with green band.
Regimental March, "I'm Ninety-five."
Allied Regiment: 6th Regiment (The Duke of Connaught's Own Rifles) of Canada.

THE RIFLE BRIGADE (The Prince Consort's Own)

Raised in 1800 the regiment saw active service before a year was out in the attack on Ferrol. A detachment was on Nelson's flagship as marines at the battle of the Baltic. Their courage was favourably commented upon at Waterloo where they rendered particularly valuable service at a critical period. In all parts of the world the Rifle Brigade have rendered devoted service to King and Country, and have fully earned and maintained the reputation that won for them the eulogy of King William IV, who said "Wherever there has been fighting, there you have been, and wherever you have been you have distinguished yourselves."

Nicknames: "The Greenjackets" and "The Sweeps."

(*Record Office*, Woolwich.)

Motto: *Nil sine labore* (Nothing without Labour).
Uniform, Blue.
Facings, White.
Head-dress, Helmet.
Cap, Blue with blue band.
Regimental March, "Wait for the Wagons."

ARMY SERVICE CORPS

The Army Service Corps has no counterpart in any European Army, and has been evolved from years of warfare in all parts of the world. The result, as proved in the great war on the Continent, is to place the Corps in the forefront of any similar service among the Allies, and the Corps has been the wonder of the armies of the world. The Corps is the outcome of experience gained in the organisation of several corps which had been formed for special purposes and afterwards disbanded. The present high standard of efficiency of the Corps is due to the fact that it has been slowly but surely recognised by Generals in command of military expeditions that the ultimate success of their operations depended primarily on the efficiency of the supply and transport service, and so with the flight of years the Corps has been grudgingly given that degree of importance in the Army it has so well merited. It has gone through many transformations from the Commissaries of Muster, Royal Waggon Train, Land Transport Corps, Military Train, and Commissariat and Transport Corps to its present designation and duties.

When it was the Military Train it was called "Moke Train." Popularly known as "The Commos."

Motto: *In Arduis Fidelis* (Faithful in Danger).
Uniform, Blue.
Facings, Dull Cherry.
Head-dress, Helmet.
Cap, Blue, with cherry-red band.
Regimental March, "Her Bright Smile."

ROYAL ARMY MEDICAL CORPS

The Corps dates its present organization from 1873 when the old regimental medical system was abolished, which had many weaknesses and was open to considerable abuse. The reorganisation has been greatly to the benefit of the whole Army for it has provided a medical service far superior in skill, organization and establishment to any medical service in the world. Not only is the professional skill of the medical officers and the nursing skill of the men the best that the nation can provide, but the sympathy and devotion to their humane duties evinced by all ranks is a theme of constant admiration, and one of the most glorious traditions of the Army. In the hottest and most dangerous areas of the battlefield, in the dread infectious wards of the hospitals, and in their care of the sick and wounded, the members of the Corps have shown a devotion and bravery that has reflected the utmost glory on the whole nation. Many of the Officers and other ranks have won the highest and most coveted decorations on the field in discharging their splendid mission of saving life.

Nicknames: "Linseed Lancers," and "Poultice Wallopers."

Uniform, Blue.
Facings, Maroon.
Head-dress, Helmet.
Cap, Blue, with maroon band.

ARMY VETERINARY SERVICE AND ARMY VETERINARY CORPS

This humane service was brought into being in 1796. Previously the treatment of equine diseases in the service had been entrusted to the farriers, zealous, but for the most part ignorant, men working by rule of thumb. The founding of the Royal Veterinary College, London, just prior to that period helped materially in putting the corps on a sound professional basis, and the diploma of the College was a *sine qua non* for a commission in the Corps. The first Veterinary Surgeon appears to have been Mr. John Ship, who was appointed to the 11th Light Dragoons in June 1796 and a few months later Professor Coleman of the Royal Veterinary College was appointed Principal Veterinary Surgeon to the Cavalry and Senior Veterinary Surgeon to the Ordnance. Under his energetic guidance the foundations of our splendidly efficient Veterinary service were laid. The service was re-organised in 1881, all regimental appointments, except those in the Household Cavalry, being abolished, and in 1891 substantive military rank was conferred on the officers instead of relative rank. The South African war brought a further development in the inclusion of N.C.O.'s and men in the Corps, and now the Corps musters a very strong body of experts whose services have been of inestimable value in the great war on the Continent.

Nicknames: "The Vets"; "The Horse Doctors."

Uniform, Blue.

Facings, Scarlet.
Head-dress, Helmet.
Cap, Blue.

ARMY ORDNANCE DEPARTMENT AND ARMY ORDNANCE CORPS

It is a remarkable fact that the Ordnance Department has a greater antiquity than any other branch of the Army, its history being traceable to the earliest military organisation of England. At one time it was a civilian department, then a branch of the Artillery, then a branch of the Engineers, and so curiously interwoven that it is very difficult to establish its actual origin. The first official record of an Ordnance Department dates back to 1418, when John Louth was appointed "Clerk to the Ordnance." The Master Bowyer, Master Fletcher, Master Carpenter, etc., were styled Officers of the Ordnance, which about 1455 became centralised at the Tower of London, where the Department continued for four hundred years under "The Master of the Ordnance," until removed to Woolwich. The duties have been, as now, closely associated with the provision and care of war-like stores, especially arms and ammunition, and the designation of the Department has varied considerably, the efficiency of the Department being steadily increased and splendidly maintained in the face of great difficulties.

Nicknamed "The Ordnance" and "The Sugar Stick Brigade" from the peculiar red and white piping of the braid.

Uniform, Blue.
Facings, Yellow.
Head-dress, Helmet.
Cap, Blue with yellow band.

ARMY PAY DEPARTMENT AND ARMY PAY CORPS

Before the establishment of the Army Pay Department in 1878, the financial side of the soldier's service was administered almost without system, this being carried out for the greater part according to the whim or skill of each commanding officer. So many people "had a finger in the pie" in handling the soldier's pay that the wonder is that any ever reached him at all, whilst the loss to the nation was enormous. After the abolition of the system under which each Colonel paid his men or did not, as he thought fit, Army Agents were made more or less responsible for paying the troops, and these appointed their own paymasters in each regiment. This system was open to abuse, and the troops suffered until the whole system of pay was taken over by the War Office and the Pay Department established. This Department also took over the payment for all the needs of the regiments and corps, and so well has it arranged its duties that every man in the army is now sure of every penny due to him, whilst the nation has been saved vast sums by preventing fraud and overcharging.

Nicknames: "The Quill Drivers" and "The Ink Slingers."

Uniform, Blue.
Facings, Red.
Head-dress, Helmet.
Cap, Red.

MILITARY POLICE

The formation of this Corps is comparatively a recent one, for until the year 1880 police duties in times of peace were discharged regimentally, and in times of war by more or less haphazard detachments under selected officers known as Provost Marshals. The formation of the Military Mounted and Foot Police, however, placed this important work on more solid and organised foundations, and in war and peace the members of the Corps discharge, in a most efficient manner, a large variety of important duties few are aware of. The policing of camps, lines of communication, supply bases and other important centres is only part of their work, which include the custody of prisoners of war, the safeguarding of general officers, and the execution of spies and other condemned prisoners.

Nickname: "The Red Caps."

"Gibraltar."
Motto: *Per Mare, per Terram* (By Sea or Land).
Uniform, Royal Marine Artillery, Blue; Royal Marine Light Infantry, Scarlet.
Facings, Royal Marine Artillery, Scarlet; Royal Marine Light Infantry, Blue.

ROYAL MARINES

The evolutions of the Marines as a separate force before the accession of Queen Anne are little known. The earliest mention of Marines as a distinct force occurs in 1664, being an Order in Council for the formation of a body of 1,200 men for the sea service. Many infantry regiments have in their early days served as Marines, but the separate Corps seems to have had a corporate existence since the date mentioned above. Splendid service has been rendered on land and sea ever since, and the Marines are as justly considered as being among the best fighting men the Empire has. Their records show them to have taken important parts in many a famous battle on land, whilst contributing their share to every victory afloat.

The Royal Marines were, by the French, nicknamed "The Little Grenadiers," from the regiment wearing Grenadier caps. They are popularly known as "The Jollies." The Corps was originally raised for sea service alone. In 1664 it bore the name of "The Admiral's Regiment" in consequence, and "Neptune's Bodyguard."

ORDERS & DECORATIONS WORN IN THE BRITISH ARMY

The following are some of the principal medals, decorations and orders that have been worn, or are worn, by British soldiers:—

War Medals.

General Service Medal, 1793-1814.
India Medal, 1799-1826.
Waterloo Medal, 1815.
First Burmah War, 1824-6.
Capture of Ghuznee, 1839.
Cabul Medal, 1843.
China War, 1842-1860.
Afghan War, 1843-3.
Sutlej Campaign, 1845-6.
New Zealand, 1846-65.
Punjaub, 1848-9.
India General Service, 1852-95.
South Africa, 1853-79.
Crimea, 1854-56.
Baltic, 1854-5.
Indian Mutiny, 1857-8.
Canada, 1866-70.
Abyssinia, 1868.
Ashanti, 1879-94.
Afghanistan, 1878-80.
Roberts Star, 1879.
Cape of Good Hope.
Egypt, 1882-89.
Khedive's Star, 1882-89.
N.W. Canada, 1885.
W. Africa, 1890-1900.
Matabeleland, 1893.
Central Africa, 1894-98.

India General Service, 1895-1898.
Ashanti Star, 1896.
Sudan (British), 1896.
Sudan (Khedive's), 1896.
East and Central Africa, 1897-99.
China, 1900.
S. Africa (Queen's), 1899-1902.
Do. (King's), 1901-2.
3rd Ashanti, 1900.
East African General Service, 1900-1904.
India General Service, 1901-02.
Tibet, 1903-04.

Orders and Decorations.

Victoria Cross.
Order of the Bath.
Order of St. Michael and St. George.
Royal Victorian Order.
The Distinguished Service Order.
The Military Cross.
Order of St. John of Jerusalem.
Albert Medal.
Territorial Officer's Decoration.
The Jubilee Decoration.
The Coronation Decoration.
Distinguished Conduct Medal.
Meritorious Service Medal.
Long Service and Good Conduct Medal.
Militia Long Service Medal.
Yeomanry Long Service Medal.
Volunteer Long Service Medal.
Territorial Force Efficiency Medal.
Royal Humane Society's Medal.
Order of Osmanieh.
Order of Mejidie.
Legion of Honour.
St. George's Medal (Russian).

CPSIA information can be obtained at www.ICGtesting.com
Printed in the USA
BVOW04s2347120616

451781BV00007B/27/P